The Amazon is Burning – The Flames of 21st Century Resistance Inspired by Indigenous Women.

I0448986

The Amazon is Burning - The Flames of 21st Century Resistance Inspired by Indigenous Women

Damon Corrie

Published by Damon Corrie, 2019.

While every precaution has been taken in the preparation of this book, the publisher assumes no responsibility for errors or omissions, or for damages resulting from the use of the information contained herein.

THE AMAZON IS BURNING - THE FLAMES OF 21ST CENTURY RESISTANCE INSPIRED BY INDIGENOUS WOMEN

First edition. October 8, 2019.

Written by Damon Corrie.

Also by Damon Corrie

Life Lessons Series
Understanding Spirituality, Anomalous Phenomena as life lessons
Understanding Spirituality, Dreams, Insights, Exorcisms, Visitations
and Shamanic Healing
Dream State Experiences

Standalone
The Amazon is Burning - The Flames of 21st Century Resistance
Inspired by Indigenous Women
Amazonia's Mythical and Legendary Creatures in the Eagle Clan
Lokono-Arawak Oral Tradition of Guyana
Lokono-Arawaks

Watch for more at https://www.facebook.com/shamanchief/.

I dedicate this book to our deceased first daughter Aderi (Little Dove), who's untimely death at 3 days old, due to medical malpractice is a direct consequence of the general apathy and discrimination of the dominant society towards to its indigenous true landlords.

I also dedicate it to my deceased brother-in-law and closest brother-friend in the tribe, Ernest Courtney Simon 'Rami', he not only helped me bury my daughter (and years later I buried him) but also without this 6 years older ex-combat veteran, and our greatest warrior of the 20th century, ever faithfully at my side in my 20s, I may have not been emboldened to have become the 'Rebel with a cause' that I am today.

True Tales from 25 years of Vigilante Activities in Defence of Native Peoples of Amazonia by the Caribbean's Most Radical Indigenous Rights Activist.

Advance Praise for:

The Amazon is Burning - The Flames of 21st Century Resistance Inspired by Indigenous Women. True Tales From 25 years of Vigilante Activities in Defence of Native Peoples of Amazonia by the Caribbean's Most Radical Indigenous Rights Activist.

"Damon Corrie tells the world a story of courage, determination, love for the land and the quest for Justice from Indigenous peoples' perspective. A story that has been intentionally ignored by the colonizers with their attempts to erase Caribbean Indigenous Peoples's place in history - but Damon's tenacity reveals that finally his peoples' story will be told."

Katsi'tsakwas Ellen Gabriel Wakeniáhton - Turtle Clan

Mohawk activist, artist, & official spokesperson for the people of the Longhouse during the 1990 Oka Crisis in Canada

"A warrior is called to sacrifice and activate liberation in all respects. Seek the sacred and chase the truth with humility".

Chase Iron-Eyes

American Indian activist, attorney, politician, and a member of the Oglala Sioux Tribe, USA.

"Refreshing, empowering...., the much needed non-apologetic stance of an Indigenous "Guaribo" Warrior in the 21st Century!"

Tai Pelletier

Human Rights, Indigenous Rights, & Environmental Rights Advocate, Puerto Rico, Caribbean

"As a young Chief of the Kalinago in Dominica 39 years ago, I experienced what it was like to become the target of an attempted coup by a hostile Caribbean Neo-Colonial government, just for re-asserting my peoples inherent rights as recognized under International Law, So I applaud brother Damon's noble and fearless efforts to bring justice to our oppressed peoples in Amazonia!"

Chief Irvince Auguiste

Most famous leader of the Kalinago Tribal Nation of Dominica island, Caribbean

INTRODUCTION

Arranged into 9 short chapters (covering political assassinations, human trafficking, illegal loggers, illegal miners, military abuses, Narco traffickers, police abuses, illegal ranchers, and invading settlers), this book gives the reader a fascinating glimpse behind the scenes into the desperate plight of native peoples of Amazonia.

Included are real-life examples drawn from the author's personal involvement in vigilante activities in defense of native peoples throughout Amazonia, spanning a period of 25 years.

Due to the sensitivity of the information presented, many names of individuals, tribes and even in some cases countries – have either been changed, or specifically omitted entirely from the text, so that the locations and persons involved cannot be discovered; for the protection of all persons involved – including the author where deemed necessary.

"The seed was sown in me in my early childhood - by my grandmother, mother, older sister, and female aunts and cousins in our Clan, because they showed me examples of strong women who did not tolerate injustice in their lives or those of their loved ones around them.

From my grandfather and father, I learned that a real mans role is to love, respect, and protect, the elders, women, and children in the family....and for US 'family' meant ALL my blood relatives and all my friends (who are my spiritual relatives).

In my pre-teen years at my first private Catholic primary school in Barbados, I had organised the boys in my class into 'my gang' by age 10, there was one kindhearted African and Indigenous mixed girl in my class (N'Della) that was unfairly picked on in my opinion, so I became her friend and protector, I used to share my lunch with her, and encouraged her to fight back and defend herself more – and she did. Then in public government Secondary school, my rebellion to authority and penchant for vigilante justice manifested itself in various ways, such as when a teacher raised his hands to strike me – so I picked up a wooden school chair to strike him back with in return, so he backed down, and he just ignored me after he saw I was not afraid to fight him.

When I noticed a group of boys were beating up weaker boys and taking their money, I organized my own group of boys, and we beat up the bullies and forced THEM to pay us 'protection money' to avoid getting beat up daily, and we gave that money to the boys they had been bullying. When we caught boys who touched girls in our school inappropriately – against their will, we just beat them up and warned them not to do it again, and forced them to apologize to the girls in question.

However, when I was 17, the Oka crisis in Canada erupted onto our nightly TV screens, and I watched my fellow indigenous relatives – the People of the Longhouse (the Six Nations Confederacy of the Iroquois), willing to fight the Canadian Armed Forces - and die in defense of their indigenous lands if necessary.

I was transfixed and greatly inspired by the fearless native Canadian women leaders like Ellen Gabriel of the Mohawk Nation, who were standing on the front lines unarmed, shoulder to shoulder with their men against the mechanized infantry of the Canadian Army with its superior weapons and greater numbers.

The next turning point in my life was in December 1992, when I married back into my tribe – and thus broke the 67-year separation caused by my family moving away from Guyana and into a voluntary exile in the Caribbean island of Barbados in 1925. My great grandmother left Guyana with her 6 surviving children because the Chiefdom of her father was no more and the few survivors scattered, as after the epidemics of the late 1800's in Guyana on tribal lands, she was literally all that was left of the bloodline of our Hereditary line of Chiefs that stretched back over 400 years., so she married out of our tribe in order to save the traditional leadership lineage from extinction. Great grandmother herself died in Barbados just 4 years later in 1928...and the long darkness that almost led to the Clan in exile becoming permanently severed from our people who were still living on the Tribal lands back in Guyana.

Learning first hand, of all the hardships my people had faced in those 67years of separation, especially our women and girls, cemented my personal conviction to do whatever I could do to help them, because it was clear that they could not depend on the Neo-Colonial powers that be – to do so; very often the powers that be were the ones inflicting misery and injustice upon them!"

These examples of some of my self-financed, organized and led vigilante activities that I share

here, are the reason why I have earned the reputation as 'the Caribbeans most radical indigenous rights activist', and I was honored recently in Barbados by the Barbados Museum and Historical Society in their Exhibition 'Insurgents – redefining rebellion in Barbados' exhibit on 8th March 2019. Few are willing to 'break the laws of the land' in order to achieve justice....but not me.

I was recently asked if I was still active in the vigilante arena, but I consider myself retired from 'active duty', preferring to focus on other pursuits for now, however, if someday in the future, I find myself living in times and circumstances that require me to return to the path of vigilante justice...then I shall not hesitate to do so again, because I have never feared any human authority figure...the only thing I have always feared is living the worthless life of a coward obsessed with hiding from danger instead of taking whatever risk that becomes necessary – in order to help someone in desperate need.

I am a warrior, and it is my nature to face danger if I believe that doing so serves a higher purpose such as saving the life of an innocent victim, and I would rather fail and die young in the attempt to help – than to live a long life as a coward who never risked his life for anyone or anything."

Lastly, I wish to thank and honor the memory of my deceased older brother-in-law and brother-friend Rami, for without him as an actual war and combat veteran (even though he was just 5 years older than me), I may not have embarked on these dangerous missions on my own, knowing that I had him ready and willing to handle any worst-case scenario emboldened me, all through the first half of my quarter-century of being a rebel WITH a cause.

CHAPTER 1 - POLITICAL ASSASSINATIONS

The first time I criticized a Government Minister of a country in South America, I was 21 years old, and it was because this Minister was the secret co-owner of the largest alcohol selling business on a tribal territory I visit.

I remember seeing little native children not even teenagers yet, buying alcohol from this establishment – all they had to say was they were buying it for an adult relative and it was sold to them (illegal in the laws of this country by the way).

So I began to openly criticize this government Minister for profiting from one of the most destructive foreign vices to ever contaminate native communities.

The most hypocritical aspect of this whole scenario was the fact that this man was himself the Minister for native peoples in this country, and he himself was a native person (married to a non-native).

Within 3 days of my public chastisement and rebuke of this Minister, he came to the village in person with his driver and bodyguards, he had heard I was exposing him and he had come to confront me in a rage.

I saw his entourage arrive, and I saw him get out of his vehicle demanding to know who I was and where I was...as if this 'how dare he' approach would have instilled fear in me or something.

All through my teenage life I NEVER started a fight, but I ALWAYS enjoyed finishing one.

The village Chief was the one who had to officially receive the Government Minister and I saw the Chief point me out to the Minister, as I was sitting only about 100 meters away, and the Chief beckoned me to come over, so I stood up and I went to them.

The Chief invited us all into the Tribal Council office and the Minister took his seat, while I took mine, with the Chief between us. Then the Minister began to rant in an angry tone.

It was clear that he assumed that because I was merely a young foreigner and he was a grown middle-aged adult Minister of the Government, that I was supposed to be very intimidated by him. Heck man, at the age of 13 I was throwing balloons filled with water at Police vehicles and getting them to chase me through urban neighborhoods just for fun...so angry words from a civil servant would hardly make me cower in fear at the age of 21.

However, I sat in respectful silence and let him speak his mind, but when he tried to overstep his legal boundaries and bluff me – that is when I decided to reply and call his bluff.

You see, he had said that I could never again enter ANY native community in his country without first sending a letter to him requesting his permission to 'allow' me to enter the community.

So I replied "I know the laws of this country concerning native peoples and YOU have no authority to grant me nor deny me permission to enter ANY native community that I visit, ONLY the village Chiefs have the power to grant or refuse me entry, so you can send the Police or Army in to arrest me whenever you want, because I will NEVER ask YOU permission to go ANYWHERE I want to in this country."

With that, he angrily stood to his feet and pointed his finger in my face shouting at me and threatening me by saying: "YOU WANT ME TO SEND YOU BACK TO BARBADOS IN A COFFIN!"

Well when he did that the gloves were off and MY temper also erupted, so I stood to my feet and pointed MY finger in his face shouting down at him (because he was at least 6 inches shorter than me) saying: "YOU JUST REMEMBER THAT IF YOU TRY TO KILL ME AND FAIL – I WILL TRY TO KILL YOU IN

RETALIATION AND I MIGHT SUCCEED! - SO GO FOR IT BIG MAN!"

With that – the Chief stood to HIS feet and parted us and told everyone to calm down, and he said the meeting is over and the Minister and I departed as bitter enemies. The Minister got back into his vehicle and they drove away.

A few days later I left that village and went to visit another tribe further into the interior, but my first night there – I had a premonition dream warning me of impending danger (a normal occurrence for me, to be forewarned in my dreams I mean).

In my dream I saw that an assassin armed with a knife hidden under the black jeans jacket he would be wearing, would come the next day looking for me, and he had been paid to kill me by the Minister....(it is not expensive in this country, give a thug US$100 and they would stab someone for you, especially in a remote location where law and order is non-existent, although if you are willing to pay US$500 or more – you can get a Policeman or soldier to shoot the person for you instead...the Minister did not want to spend too much on me it seems, the cheapskate).

So at dawn, before my hosts roused from their slumber, I slipped away into the jungle and followed another path to a remote fishing camp I knew, that was very difficult terrain to track someone over. I laid low at the location, and spend 2 days there before returning to the village.

When I returned, my host the Chief and his family were surprised to see me saying they thought the Jungle had taken me because I was suddenly gone, but they had expected that I would be staying for a few days (that is when I realized someone in the village was a snitch and had relayed my plans to be there back to the Minister), so I just laughed and give a vague and mystical reply as I know they were a superstitious family, but what the Chief said next confirmed once again the accuracy of my premonition dreams of warning.

The Chief said: "A man came here looking for you yesterday morning, not long after you disappeared, he said he was an old friend of yours and he came to pay you a surprise visit, he stayed all day and slept here up till last night, but could not wait any longer and left this morning early, he never gave us his real name though, just that they call him 'squaddie'..do you know him?" ....so I asked: "Was he wearing a black jeans jacket?" - the Chief's wife replied, "Yes – how do you know?"...so I just laughed. 'Squaddie' is a common false name for a man who was formerly in the Army or Police Force in that country.

So I left that village safely as I entered it, but I decided to retaliate in a non-violent way against that Minister, I sent a report to a Human Rights body, whose head had contacts high in the UN, about the Ministers threat to kill me – (and of course I did not mention my threat to try to kill him as well in retaliation IF he did so), the Report reached all the way to the desk of the Secretary-General, whos office sent it to that countries UN diplomatic mission, who then sent it to the President of the country, who in turn felt very embarrassed that it had come from the office of the Secretary-General and FIRED the Minister (who was unpopular anyway even within his own political party). The Minister became an alcoholic himself in his unemployment, and he has since died powerless and penniless.

I should have warned him of the old phenomenon (some call it a curse upon our enemies) in my family, because every time someone tries to physically harm or actually causes physical harm to any member of our bloodline, the perpetrator either becomes physically hurt or killed themselves or they lose everything they had in life.

Unfortunately, 17 other indigenous friends I have known over the years in various countries of Amazonia, were not so lucky, because they were all murdered by assassins on the payroll of politicians, or rich unscrupulous business-men – for standing up for the rights of native peoples against government projects, illegal miners, illegal loggers, human traffickers, drug traffickers etc. Many were tortured before being killed as well.

CHAPTER 2 - HUMAN TRAFFICKING

Incident #1 NATIVE GIRL HELD IN FORCED PROSTITUTION

Rami (my now deceased former right-hand-man) and I were in that city, we saw a young native woman being beaten in public by her non-native man, other people watched and laughed but no-one helped.

We were outnumbered and unarmed, so no on-the-spot intervention, we had to bide our time.

He left with his friends, she was alone and crying, I told Rami to go to her and ask her if she wanted our help, she did, she wanted to escape from her 'man', she was pregnant, 7 months or thereabouts I reckon, said he beat her often, kicked her in the stomach and made her lose their first child, and forced her to let his friends have sex with her when he was high on drugs.

This non-native man who now had her as his sex slave, had entered her Tribal Village as a miner from a nearby camp 2 years before, and had convinced her and her family that he was madly in love with her, and he was going to give her a better life and send money to help her parents to improve their home and take better care of the many other younger siblings.

So being the typical 'always trusting and seeing the good in others' - but also desperately poor – native people, they believed his lies. Thus, they let their daughter leave her community with a man they thought was her Prince Charming.

We found out where she lived and told her to be ready to move immediately when she saw us again - which could be at any time. We had close-shaved heads and clean-shaven faces at that time, we really looked the part as soldiers; so I bought complete military uniforms on the black market, no guns this time though, and we pretended to be

Soldiers, so Rami and I went out in public in our fake identity, walked past a real policeman, even he was fooled (in this country the Soldiers have more authority than the Police – so the Police cannot arrest a real soldier) but it was a close call, had we been discovered to only be imitating real soldiers we would have received 10 years in jail each - as punishment.

We hailed a taxi and told him to drive to the bad part of town to the address we had been told, I told the taxi driver to "wait for us with the engine running" the taxi driver also thought we were soldiers, Rami knocked on the door, the man opened, Rami asked him if (her name) lived there, I was playing the 'commanding officer' role, the man said yes, I then said we have a warrant for her arrest and produced a convincing (to a semi-literate criminal thug like him) document for him to read as we pushed past him into the house, it had many official-looking stamps on it – all fake stamps I paid to get made – in order to pull off this rescue mission by making it look more convincing.. The LAST thing any criminal wants is to stand in the way of an 'official investigation' that had the Chief of Police AND the President's signature on it. We found her and I told her: "Pack your bag you have to come with us".

In a flash I collected back the fake document I had created and we were out the door with her and told the taxi driver take us straight to the airport, when we reached I had enough money to buy her a one-way plane ticket back to her home village, where she would be safe with her tribe and family. She hugged both of us and with tears running down her face she said goodbye and we never saw her again.

Incident 2 NATIVE GIRLS PEDOPHILE RING

In order to get into a restricted area in a certain country to document abuses against native teenaged girls by alleged pedophile business owners, Rami and I used the Army uniforms that I had purchased on the black market before.

Rami and I were in a civilian bus (back seat), a paramilitary checkpoint halted the vehicle, one of the Paramilitaries with an assault rifle boarded the bus and told everyone to "Get off the bus and show some form of ID", Rami and I did not move, we figured the gig was up now, as we had the look but no official form of military ID, and I was not sure if the Paramilitary forces had more authority than the Police or not, this was a new scenario.

The Paramilitary with his assault rifle boarded the bus again to make sure everyone had complied with his order, he sees Rami and I in the back seat dressed like regular Army Soldiers, the Paramilitary salutes us, we salute him back, he leaves the bus and tells the 'civilians' to get back on board, Soldiers, evidently - are higher ranking than paramilitaries ALSO so he thought we were his superiors.

So we reached the settlement, it was a non-native settlement but inhabited mostly by poor natives from the area, it was dominated by 3 bars that sold all the liquor, and purchased all the diamonds and gold from the small scale wildcat operators in the region.

The 3 bar owners running this settlement were routinely preying on the desperately poor illiterate young native girls, Rami and I sat in little local bars at night watching them and listening to them.

They would get drunk and talk about which girl (not women as these were all underaged children) they had sex with last, and which one had a 'tighter hole' than another, they had raped many virgins from what we heard, some even bragged about 'naked skin birthday parties' where they passed around little native girls for the non-native men to have sex with one after the other, they complained that these little girls were not very good in bed because they did not know about oral sex and they often had to be beaten because they were so uncooperative with the non-native men who were raping them. One non-native woman who owned a bar in this place was even raping little girls herself, the men laughed about catching her using a strap-on on a girl who was screaming in pain.

The saddest thing was hearing that the parents were aware of their daughters being abused but were so terrified of being killed if they said or tried to do anything, that they suffered in silence when you are poor and powerless, and you have been brainwashed by an ultra-pacifist "Offer no resistance to injury" colonialism manipulated religious ideology....this is the kind of end result crap that happens, fathers and mothers too afraid to take vigilante justice into their own hands and defend their children no matter what. If it was me, and this had happened to my daughter, I would have killed all of them – and felt proud to have ridden the earth of such scum. Most killings go unsolved after all.

As the night wore on I was getting more upset, as I could not imagine that the horrors we were hearing were actually happening to innocent little girls like this. So before we left I said to Rami:

"We can't just leave here with names and reports, you heard what the manager said, the Chief of Police is his personal friend and was at one of these naked skin parties, you think our reports will achieve anything? No dread, we have to fuck-up these people ourselves, because no-one else here seems to have the guts to do it.

To explain a bit more about Rami, he was my brother-in-law. So I had no fear of him betraying me, because it would not benefit him to do so, he would only be hurting his sister (my wife) and his nephews and nieces (our children), so I let people like him into my inner circle of vigilante activities because their loyalty is not a risk to me, neither was he ambitious, he was happy to support me in all my plans, never the type to want to take over the leadership and do things differently. I revealed my plans to him, and he volunteered to join me in carrying them out, as he lived without fear either...as he himself was an actual veteran of the Suriname civil war in the jungle interior of that country, where he killed many enemies, so my vigilante activities were child's play to him.

It just so happened that December 31st was going to be the very next night, and I calculated that with all the explosions at midnight and people gathered en masse at a central open-air spot to watch the fireworks show, it would be the perfect time to conduct an economic sabotage operation, we had been there a few days and had acquired enough gasolene to do what I had in mind.

Sure enough, Old Years night/New Year's Eve came and most all the residents were gathered on the soccer field to watch the fireworks show, luckily it was not such a big target area to cover, the 3 bars where the girls were being abused in the back rooms were all close to each other.

BY 11.45 pm just about everyone was there, including the ringleaders who were sponsoring the fireworks show and taking turns acting as the MCs

It gave Rami and I enough time to verify no-one was in the buildings, and soak the backs of their wooden buildings and all their vehicles with gasoline (wearing latex gloves that I later discarded into the fire of course), we waited until the fireworks display began as Rami was on lookout to make sure no-one was coming our way one last time, he signaled me that the coast was clear, and I lit the bars and vehicles on fire, then we melted away into the bush, doubled back around to the field, and joined the crowd of spectators as if nothing happened, by the time the magnificent fireworks show was over about 12.10 am, the bars and the bar owners vehicles were all raging infernos and the crowd had rushed over to them trying to help out the flames – as we did so too, you have to keep up the act, after all, the main ringleader was literally in tears because he had all his money in cash in his bar and was planning to take it out in 2 days time to put in the bank, he lost all the stock he had just received that day which he was going to sell all through this night, the other 2 including the woman pedophile were also in tears, apparently they did not

trust the banks to keep their money safe, so their life savings were in their bars – which also doubled as their homes as well, hence the back rooms with beds etc, where they committed most of their crimes.

These disgusting criminals really thought we were their 'new friends', and all the while I was speaking words of incredulity and comfort to them – such as:

"I can't believe this, how could such a thing happen...all your life savings gone just like that, so sad man" etc...in my MIND I was laughing my head off – and thinking to myself "Taste the karmic justice for raping all those children you fuckers!". Long story short, those 3 formerly successful pedophile bar owners were reduced to poverty overnight...oh how the mighty hath fallen...and they never reopened any business there again, I sent reports the various human rights and media entities anonymously, mentioning what was going on and that the bar owner 'claimed' they had the protection of the Chief of Police, so that gave the top cop the wiggle room to distance himself (now that they could no longer afford to bribe him – so were no longer useful to him) and order an investigation, last I heard the bar owners were on the run and never heard from nor seen since.

Incident 3 – HOW TO USE UN GIFT SHOP SOUVENIRS TO SAVE LIVES

Now here is one example everyone can try for themselves, especially if you do not have the stomach to use violent (albeit non-lethal as no-one died) tactics like my example in incident 2

I have been a registered participant at the United Nations since 2007, and I realized very early on, from my extensive background in vigilante activities, that items in the official United Nations Gift Shop inside UN headquarters - as simple (and cheap to buy) as blue baseball caps with the UN logo, and white T-shirts with the UN logo, and having pens, notebooks, and bags with the UN logo - could become very useful to me as disguises that would allow me to rescue indigenous people in need of help, because to the average policeman or soldier (and also the person on the street), if they see someone dressed up in all that UN stuff – they ASSUME you must be a UN employee.

The only thing you need to make it more convincing is a temporary UN photo ID ...the kind all of us who attend the UNPFII every year routinely get, but 99% of us ONLY use it the way it was officially meant to be used for...that is – just to get into UN headquarters daily for 2 weeks once a year. That is because most of my fellow IP delegates don't think outside of the box, you don't see how simple items like these can be used to OUR advantages....but I do.

Mind you, I NEVER say 'Yes I work for the UN" (as I never was a UN employee nor have I ever been paid any salary by the UN) if asked, I answer truthfully by saying I have been a registered participant at the United Nations Permanent Forum on Indigenous Issues since 2007 "...and that answer seems good enough to satisfy whatever doubt or curiosity that exists in their uneducated minds at the moment in time. Usually, they never ask me anything, they just ASSUME by the way I look...hey, if it works and you can save an innocent life – by all means, do it. That is my philosophy anyway.

I can share this idea with you now, because if I get banned from the UN because of my revelations in this book, even though I am helping people most in need, I can still get friends to buy these souvenirs at the UN gift shop for me to continue what I was doing, and if I have to, I have enough old UN photo ID's from my 10 years there – that I can pay to have a very good fake UN I made for myself, and the kinds of police and military authorities in remote areas, I deal with on rescue missions throughout Amazonia won't have a damned clue if my new (privately made) UN ID is legit or not.

And now the incident:

I once heard that a racist non-native policeman (with a reputation for brutality and framing native men for crimes they did not commit) had illegally assaulted and arrested a native man and took him to the nearby border Police Station, so I put on my 'UN disguise' and I went there. As soon as I entered the station I asked for the commanding officer and I introduced myself (in my UN attire of course), I told them I was just passing through the area and I had received an urgent complaint by native leaders about a native man who had just been physically assaulted, illegally detained, arrested and transported off of his Tribal Lands by one of his lower-ranked officers – in violation of the constitution of the country as it relates to the rights of native persons – which requires the consent of the Chief of the village before a native community member may be transported away in Police custody, I spoke with confidence and authority as if I really WAS a UN official, however, I never SAID I was any such thing so legally speaking I did nothing wrong, I then went on to tell the Commanding officer, a Sargeant I believe, that if the young native man was not released immediately I would have no choice but to submit a report to my boss (and here is where I added dramatic exaggeration) "who would then send it to the UN Secretary General, who would then send it to the President, who would then send it to Chief of Police, who may feel that in order to save personal embarrassment and show that he was dealing with the matter decisively...may see fit to make an example of someone, and you are the one in charge here so most likely that scape-goat would be you".

This was enough to put the 'fear of career complications' into the Police Sargeant, and he immediately became apologetic, he angrily summoned the lower-ranked officer who had illegally arrested the native man, and publicly chastised him in front of me much to my personal amusement), telling him such things as:

"What you arrested the man for? Do you know you were in violation of his rights to arrest him and remove him from his village without the consent of the Chief? What is wrong with you? You turn stupid or what? Release that man right away!" Furthermore, apologies to the man for roughing him up too, you know we don't tolerate the abuse of prisoners in the Force!"

I made sure to let the Policemen in the station see me writing their names down in my UN notebook with my UN pen and I said to the Sargeant for all of them to hear:

"We have been getting serious complaints about officers from this station routinely violating the human rights of native peoples, my superiors will be keeping a close eye on this station from now on, I trust that your Sargeant will be keeping a close eye on rogue elements that could bring dishonor and disgrace on your government in the eyes of the International community."

The native man was freed and shook my hands outside, and we went our separate ways.

See how simple that was? And all it required was the creative use of UN souvenir apparel as life-saving tools. I have not heard any further complaints of Police brutality from that station in all the years since.

On another less dramatic occasion, I was at a Police checkpoint being processed, wearing my UN attire at the time, when an old native lady tugged on my shirt and asked me if the UN could help her, she pointed at two teenaged native girls who were passing us in the opposite direction heading towards the city (we were in a separate line being processed to head further into the interior), she said that non-native man with them is known to recruit native girls in poor villages with promises as work as maids in wealthy homes, but the girls who went with him ended up in brothels.

So I assured her that yes indeed the UN is very opposed to human trafficking in all forms (which IS 100% true) and that I would help her in this case since I was there in person.

When it was my turn to reach the Policeman at the desk I pointed the two girls out in the other line and told him (with dramatic exaggeration again):

"Officer you see that non-native gentleman over there with those two legally underaged native girls, he is under an INTERPOL investigation for the sex trafficking of native girls from the interior to the cities, and this case is being followed up by your President. Minister of Justice, and the Chief of Police, it would reflect very badly on you and the other officer processing that line, if those girls are allowed by you here today to leave with a human trafficker, but it would look very good at the end of the investigation if you rescued those girls and saw that they were repatriated to their home villages, I would expect such an action on your part may lead to a special commendation – even a promotion, but again, I am only tipping you off because I think you officers deserve to be recorded as having done your jobs to the best of your abilities and be held as role models in the force in the media."

The Officer looked at the girls and the man in question, and I could see that he was pondering my words, he then told me: "Ok hold on a minute", and he called out to his other officer colleague in the other line saying:

"Hey, you checked all 3 of their papers carefully? The other officer said they looked ok to him, so the one I spoke to asked to see their papers himself.

Turns out the guy had a valid ID, but not the girls, just some hand-written note from their parents saying they gave the man permission to escort them to the city for legal employment.

So the officer I spoke to, who looked to be older than the other officer, said:

"what stupidness is this? These girls don't have any valid ID, this letter can be written by anyone, where is the stamp and signature from the Village Chief verifying the statement of these girls ages? They look younger than 18 to me, let the man continue on his way but the girls cannot accompany him until this matter is investigated further".

The man knowing he was guilty did not object to losing the 2 girls, he went on about his journey, albeit looking angry and upset about losing the 2 girls.

In case the Police were in cahoots with the trafficker and were planning to send them later to him after I had left, I asked the girls which village they came from, and when they told me I remembered that was going to be the 3rd village I was going to be passing through next over the course of this day.

So I told the officers that myself and the old lady from their same village would escort the girls back home, and so we took them with us, I bought them lunch and drinks on the way as the man did not leave any money in their hands, granny too was fed and included in our happy quartet that day.

I made sure I used the time together with them to tell them of all the deceptions and dangers of the outside world, and that they should not trust non-natives as easily as they trusted members of their own native village, these people are not like us I told them, they are like walking gold-painted coffins, they look nice on the outside, but eventually, you realize it is fake, and the only thing they have inside to offer you - is your own destruction and death.

ONE IMPORTANT TIP I WILL GIVE YOU

Is NEVER try to use a UN outfit in the Middle East thinking it will help you, I tried that ONCE when I went to help a tribe there, only made things worse for me, the security forces and governments of the Middle East generally speaking give you a HARDER time if you look like a UN employee – NOT easier, you literally only make things worse for yourself if you try this there. I can't say for Asia or Africa, but in Latin America and the Caribbean, the UN 'look' works.

CHAPTER 3 – LOGGERS

My favorite vigilante incident with illegal loggers is the one below, because no-one was hurt on our side OR the illegal loggers' side.

It happened one day on one of the training missions I was running with Rami for three other native men who had recently joined the paramilitary outfit I had created, at that time I could afford to create my own private paramilitary force, and so I did.

We were on a training patrol on Tribal lands, all of us in military uniforms of the type the special forces in that country wore, because once before it had happened that a REAL Army helicopter had surprised us by flying low overhead of the jungle canopy, and we barely had a few seconds to spare to dive into the foliage and conceal ourselves, because we had on a different type of military uniform and to the Helicopter crew (from the real Army) we would have looked like guerrillas or narco-traffickers, as we were wearing camouflage but all carrying big green duffle bags...not of drugs (but it sure would have looked so to a real Army helicopter crew) – but actually of native arts and crafts that we were taking out of one village to sell in a border town to raise money to buy more military uniforms, to expand my force there.

Anyway, so this time we were wearing the uniform of the special forces of the country we were now in, because from the air any military or police aircraft crews would have assumed (I calculated) – that we were just a special forces patrol, and by the time they went through all the military channels to verify if the 'special forces' were on any secret mission operating in that area, we would be long gone, melted safely away into the jungle, by the time any helicopter landed troops to confront or arrest us, so I decided it was a tactical move that gave us the benefit of the doubt, or a necessary strategic time advantage to escape – either way, we had the leg up.

We heard the sound of chainsaws from very far away, you cant hide and cut down trees, you can be heard from very far away, so we spread out and flanked the logging camp, rushing in on them from all sides, we had only training weapons on us. Legally purchased Air Rifles, but only the butts of the rifles were unsheathed so the loggers could not tell if they were firearms or not.

I had an Air pistol in my hand (playing the role of commanding officer again) and I shouted 'HANDS UP" as I strode into the camp, every man put down what he was doing and stood with their hands raised, "FORM A LINE! " I again barked at them with my Air pistol in my hand ...

Again they complied, my goodness it was a lot of them in this camp, at least 15 of them – so they outnumbered us 3 to one, I asked to see any firearms they had in the camp, and one man with trembling hands brought out a 20 gauge shotgun they used to hunt wild meat, in order to supplement camp rations, I checked his gun license and it was a legal weapon (I had to play my role convincingly you know lol), I also inspected their box of shogun cartridges and gave them back.

Let me see your permits to cut wood on this land, I next demanded.

The camp foreman who owned the shotgun said they did not have the paper with them, only the boss kept that, and he would not be back for another week. So knowing where they were I replied to him:

"Sir, you are lying to me, your boss could NOT have any legal paper to cut wood here – because you are on demarcated native lands, and only the Chief and Council could grant you such a permit, and we know for a fact that he did not – because he recently complained to us about illegal logging activities going on in this area, that is why the President sent us out on patrol here to investigate (these idiots do not know that the President has nothing to do with ordering the special Forces to do anything). We should arrest you all right now and take you into custody.

The foreman begins to stutter nervously, and begs to be forgiven and released, as well as the rest of the illegal loggers, I tell them I will confer with my men and see what they decide to do .." so I talk with my men and we pretend to be angry and keep a straight face, when we really and truly wanted to burst out laughing as they genuinely were in fear of us, not realizing it was THEY who could have performed a citizens arrest of US...had they realized we were illegally impersonating members of the Armed Forces.

So I returned to the line of nervous men and rendered our decision...they had to cease all logging activities, destroy the camp, and leave the area by daybreak the following day, and never to return to the area. They also had to paddle us in their boat to the nearest next village, 3 hours boat ride away, so some of the loggers had to transport us further upriver in their boat, with 2 of them paddling while we relaxed and enjoyed the free ride.

On the way the two young non-native men asked us a lot of questions, I just looked at them stern-faced (for lingering dramatic effect), and the youngest recruit of my men (Buddy) – who had a sharp wit, piled on the stories in replies to the two conscripted paddlers....when they asked about our unit and if we saw action before, he would laugh and tell them how many criminals we had killed in shoot-outs in the wilderness, and had buried the bandits in shallow graves in remote areas that no-one ever found.

He also told them we were thinking about killing them too but decided to give all of them a chance this time, but if we found them there again when we passed back on patrol we would not show them any mercy, but had agreed to kill all of them next time..(of course we never planned to do them any harm in actual fact)...the 2 'conscripts' got real silent after that, and paddled noticeably harder for the rest of the way LOL.

IN ANOTHER INCIDENT WE SCARED OFF ILLEGAL LOGGERS WITH PYROTECHNICS

There was this other time, when we had no guns, only military uniforms and lots of fireworks I like to use for training new recruits, because they give off very loud explosions, and a lot of smoke with a big flash, so very good to get new recruits used to the sounds of war, as you don't want people who get afraid when gunshots are going off – and bullets are whizzing past you, to lose courage and wimp-out on you at a critical moment.

This group of loggers had at least 2 shotgun-toting guards in it, but nonetheless, I figured that by using glue to stick the entire outside of some very powerful rockets with 1 inch headless nails, would give us just as much 'wounding' power as their shotguns would give them, plus we could stay way out of effective shotgun range and bathe them in shrapnel if we needed to, as these rockets easily doubled and tripled OUR effective range VS their shotgun ranges.

We used PVC pipes to set up what I like to call 'Multiple rocket launchers' (because it sounds more dramatic), and we were using all legally acquired weapons as fireworks were legal to purchase in that country, as were 1-inch lead nails and the glue...I just got creative with them.

When we were ready, I signaled for the first barrage to fire, a salvo of about 48 rockets landed in the loggers camp and exploded, it threw them into panic and confusion, but sure enough the 2 guys who had shotguns began to fire wildly into the bush, not knowing where the explosion that just woke them up had come from; and the thick smoke and smell of gunpower hindered them.

So I motioned for a second salvo to be fired, and this time the loggers who had the shotguns dropped them and ran away onto the savanna with the other unarmed loggers who were running for their lives....to make sure they did not come back I told the men with me (my 'troops') to begin shouting with me (for the 'enemy' to hear): "KILL THEM! KILL ALL OF THEM!"

This was purely for dramatic effect – to make sure those frightened men kept running away LOL. As the only salvo left was the shrapnel rockets, but I really did not want to hurt these men.

In ALL my 25 years of vigilante activities, I have been shot at on multiple occaissions, threatened mith assassination, and had a few attempts on my life, but all failed, and I literally have never even been physically bruised by my enemies.

Why was I so lucky – and others not? I do not know for certain, I only know that I BELIEVE that I came to this lifetime with a higher puprose, and that is to place the laws of God higher in my heart than the laws of men, and many other souls came here to do this before me, ever heard of Oscar Schindler? He was a rich German who saved thousands of Jews by breaking ALL the laws of Nazi Germany, because it was LEGAL to kill the Jews – but ILLEGAL to help them, this is an example of why the laws of GOD are superior to the laws of men. We are not here to watch the sufferring of others and do nothing, we must take any risks necessary to help each other if we are to be counted as true human beings and IF we can do this without having to take the lives of others, as the ultimate last resort, then this is a path we should be proud to walk on.

CHAPTER 4 - MINERS

In my favorite memory of native vigilante action against unscrupulous miners, it was in Brazil, can't hide it as it is the only Portuguese speaking country in South America and I don't speak Portuguese, I depend on native allies and friends to act as my interpreter.

I Spanish countries I can handle myself well enough.

I can afford to mention myself and this country in this case, because technically I did not actually do anything personally that could be classified as a crime.

Tribal friends invited me over to be 'military advisor' to an operation they had planned themselves, against some miners who were polluting their river lifeline with mercury contamination and excess silt, as they were washing away precious soil in their search for diamonds and gold. One child had been born deformed as a result of mercury poisoning already.

And just as I had personally witnessed with my own eyes by miners on the upper Demerara River in Guyana in the 1990's, here also in Brazil the graves and skeletal remains of native peoples were being washed away callously into the river – by the missile dredge mining operation that was eating up the Earth looking for precious stones and minerals.

My usefulness to my allies was by taking care of their surveillance requirements, I accompanied the group of 30 warriors they had mustered, and when they tracked down the miners camp, I used my binoculars to keep the camp under observation by day.

Then, when night fell, I took out my night vision binoculars that I bought in the USA, and two of them took me close to the miners camp so I could spy on them in total darkness, without them ever knowing we were there.

We crouched in the nearby bushes and saw that there ware only 3 Garimpeiros in this camp and only one had a hunting rifle, so I waited until the one with the gun went to bathe in a shallow stream nearby, and when he rested his rifle against a tree near his pile of clothes, I took it and gave it to one of the warriors with me, on the way back to report what we had observed he dropped it in the river at a deep bend, so it could not be used against us tomorrow when we attacked them with our bows and arrows.

We roused early and made it to the miners to surprise attack them at sunrise before they could react. The warriors had on body paint and as the leader let out a loud war cry – the others unleashed a barrage of carefully aimed arrows that landed NEAR and all around the sleeping miners, the miners jumped to their feet in fear and had the look of sheer terror on their faces.

One of the Garimpeiros actually pissed his pants in fright and tried to run away, but a warrior caught him and slapped him up a bit, then brought him back, he was crying and begging for his life. From this point on I was just a casual observer enjoying the show.

As was later explained to me in English, the warriors chastised the men verbally and slapped some sense into them, telling them how dare they come to their beautiful jungle to make it ugly trying to get riches for themselves.

The warriors told them the animals and the plants were crying out to them (the warriors) for justice because of all the evils the miners were doing in the name of money.

The warriors told them all the centuries and generations of their people who had lived in these jungles and not disturbed it – and now outsiders were defiling these sacred lands, and they would be stopped with mercy, or be stopped with vengeance, today they would show them mercy, but if they ever returned, they would be shown no mercy – only wrath.

I understood the final part when the head warrior told them in Portuguese "We do not invade your homes and destroy it looking for riches, how dare you come into our home and do this! You are lucky we let you live today!"

ALL the mining equipment was destroyed, and the camp was burned to the ground, all the miners were left with was the clothes on their backs, and a small boat to leave the area immediately and return to their town beyond the tribal territory.

I left this tribe via an Andean country, However, I was detained there by the security forces in that neighboring Spanish country, they assumed I was doing some illegal activity, as they found the night vision binoculars in my bag, but luckily I had a letter from the Embassy of their country saying I did not require a VISA to enter that country at any point because I was 'doing research on native peoples that often required traveling incognito in remote areas' (because it is not WHAT you know that counts most at such times, it is WHO you know, and I obtain useful favors from friends and supporters in positions of power and authority), so I only spent one night in a cell...looking out at the snow-capped Andes, and imagining what Che Guevara must have felt like...as he looked out of his Andean jail all those decades ago, before he was executed.

After they released me the next day and I boarded my flight at the airport, OUT of that country, I laughed to myself in relief of the completion of another successful 'military operation' by someone who was never in any military LOL....and, I remembered the many times when close friends who know what I do – had told me I am living a closer life to a James Bond movie than anyone else they ever met.

CHAPTER 5 – MILITARY ABUSES OF NATIVE PEOPLES

I know of cases where the non-native commanding officers in the military of a certain country, routinely discriminate against ANY native soldier in their Army that does better than the non-native soldiers.

In some cases these native soldiers who out-perform the others, get harassed and intimidated to go AWOL, then they are jailed and dishonorably discharged from the army...or in the worst cases, they are murdered or die in orchestrated accidents....like one friend of mine who was ordered to climb a Coconut tree in the pouring rain by a Colonel who was jealous of him being the best recruit at everything, and my friend slipped and fell from the wet tree trunk near the top and broke his neck when he hit the ground, dying instantly.

The Officer denied ordering him to climb the tree in the rain and nothing was done to punish him in any way.

In another case I personally know of, a young native soldier was outscoring all the non-native recruits in marksmanship skills, he even beat the scores of the non-native Army sniper training them, one night he was blindfolded and severely beaten in his bunk by unknown assailants, they hit him so severely in the head he was brain damaged and mentally unstable ever since the incident, so he was discharged from the Army.

Mysteriously none of his other non-native recruits in that whole room 'heard or saw anything' and no-one was punished for that crime.

Soldiers on patrol in remote areas, and soldiers living in bases in or near-native communities ALL over Amazonia - are NOTORIOUS for beating native men, and raping native girls.

These non-native soldiers are among the WORST kinds of racists against native peoples, because they have guns and uniforms that they think gives them permission to treat natives any damn way they feel like, and they know 99% of the time they WILL get away with their crimes.

Their racist anti native superiors' idea of 'punishment' is just to move the guilty soldier to another base, where he can abuse a new set of natives all over again.

They see native girls or even women WITH their boyfriends or husbands, heck even with their fathers and grandfathers, brothers or uncles, and they still show them no respect, as they say sexually suggestive things about the shape of the girl's body, her buttocks, breasts, etc and what they would like to do to those body parts, and as soon as the girl or her companion say anything to the soldiers they get shouted at and threatened in their own home villages or even beaten...

I have heard soldiers shouting vulgarities at a 13-year-old girl, and her grandfather who merely told them "You should show her a little respect she is just a girl"....was threatened by one soldier who shouted: "Who the fuck are you talking to the old man? You better mind your own fucking business before I plant my foot up in your old ass!"

I have seen native elders being shoved and slapped in their faces, boyfriends, and brothers and husbands get beat up – while soldiers fondled their female companion laughing – as the native female cried and begged them to stop.

In Guyana, they have a very disgusting non-native saying that common men often repeat and it is: "After 12 is lunch" (they say this to explain – in their spiritually dead minds) - why they see nothing wrong with having sex with girls from the age of 12 and older.

These same low caliber non-native men also think that they are not gay if they have anal sex with another man, only if someone has anal sex with THEM do they think that is 'Gay' behavior! LOL What idiots.

INCIDENT OF MILITARY ABUSE ON OUR OWN TERRITORY

My wife's cousin 'Sugar' was doing small scale logging to build a house for himself and his wife, and their children, his son Ken was helping him.

An Army patrol of ten non-native soldiers surprised them and held them at gunpoint, the father and his 12-year-old son.

Sugar had permission in writing in his possession from the Chief of our village to cut the trees, the Soldiers looked at it but did not care.

They accused Sugar of 'knowing where Ganja (aka Marijuana) farming was going on in the tribal territory and demanded he tell them where and who was doing it.

Sugar told them honestly that he did not know about any Ganja farming on the Tribal territory, but that was not the answer the racist non-native soldiers wanted to hear.

In front of his little – now traumatized son - they made Sugar lie down in the dirt, and all ten of the soldiers took turns marching across his back with their heavy Army boots.

They did this until Sugar fainted. Then they tied his wrists together and suspended him by a rope he had in his own camp, from a nearby tree.

Then, with his little son still watching and crying his eyes out begging them to "please don't kill my daddy!" ...all ten of the soldiers took turns punching him, slapping him, and lashing him with items they found in his camp.

All the while Sugar was pleading his innocence and begging them to show him mercy in front of his son.

Sugar and his forever emotionally scarred son Ken had to endure one whole day of merciless torture. Even though:

#1 - The laws of Guyana say it is ILLEGAL for the Army to patrol on Tribal Lands without informing the Village Chief and obtaining consent FIRST.

AND

#2 – The laws of Guyana say it is illegal for Soldiers to torture anyone for any reason.

And then these kinds of government soldiers wonder why native peoples HATE them so much.

CHAPTER 6 - NARCO-TRAFFICKERS – OPEN HUNTING

Now, when dealing with drug traffickers, you can get REALLY creative, they cant go to the Police to report what you did to them so it's open hunting if you have to do battle against them, however, bear in mind as well – that they know they are ALREADY wanted criminals so they have nothing to lose either, and they WILL kill your whole family...IF they find out who you are.

So naturally, I will just tell you of the first incident I heard about in any native conflict with Drug traffickers...because I knew the victim personally.

Granpa Dredis' savage murder

One time when non-native Marijuana farmers (we called Bandar's) were encroaching on our native territory, they were spotted by old native grandfather 'Dredi', he was a sort of tribal policeman, as he had been given the power to arrest people who committed non-violent offenses, but he was old, and he was never issued with any weapon by the Police Force.

Grandpa Dredi bravely (or foolishly) warned these non-native Marijuana growers that if they did not move their operation off the tribal lands, he would be forced to report their presence to the Police (who I suspect we're probably on these criminals protection payroll already anyway, but that's just my opinion). They said nothing to him, and a few days passed and folks in the tribe realized they had not seen Grandpa Dredi for a few days.

So a few of his relatives paddled their canoes up-river to his house, as old Dredi lived on the border of the territory, far from the safety of the main village, and closer to the danger of the criminal Bandar's Marijuana farming operation.

Old grandpa Dredi saw himself as the last warrior defending the furthermost outpost of the realm – of our tribes 240 square mile territory.

His family members found his tiny body (as he was less than 5 feet/ 150cm tall) floating in the river in front of his house.

'Someone' had beaten him like a rug, black and blue marks all over his body, and he had been stabbed all about his body over 70 times, and the killer/s had even cut his tongue out; because the killers had a belief that his spirit would not be able to tell anyone who conjured him to ask who had killed him.

As fate would have it, his little grandson who was visiting him at the time, witnessed it all, and he said it was the Bandar's who murdered his grandfather, he was hiding in the jungle and watched everything...that boy is a man now, but still deeply psychologically scarred by the atrocity he witnessed as a child...imagine watching your own loving, peaceful old grandfather being brutally tortured and murdered in front of your eyes, and there is absolutely nothing you can do to save him.

Dredi was the Great Great Uncle, brother of the great grandmother of my wife, but we do not call anyone a 'great uncle' or 'great aunt' in the tribe, the siblings of your grandparents are called your OTHER Grandparents.

Likewise, the siblings of your Great-grandparents are also called your grandparents, So Dredi was one of my children's grandfathers.

My children once asked me "Dad how come we have so many grandparents?" So I gave them the Tribal explanation I just gave you.

I asked the male family members what they were going to do about it, because I wanted to be part of any retaliation they were going to launch. Rami was ready to lead the attack.

We had planned and agreed that all the Bandars in the Marijuana farm were guilty of killing Grandfather, as the boy said it was all of them, and they like to share the guilt of their crimes among all members

– so no one is tempted to snitch on the others, guilt by association I guess.

So we imagined each of them taking their turn stabbing the old man a few times, hence over 70 wounds.

So we had made a pact to kill EVERY Bandar we found in their camp in a surprise attack, and feed their remains to the vultures in tiny pieces...so no evidence would ever be found, should anyone ever bother to investigate the deaths of some of the most wanted criminals in Guyana.

But at that time I was very young and newly married into their family, and I did not have enough money to finance the kind of revenge strike that would be required – if it were to be successful.

As to match the Bandars arsenal we would have needed to buy AK-47's (US$2,500 each with 100 rounds) on the black market, and I could not afford the prices quoted at that time.

However, as fate would have it again, a few days later a British warship paid a courtesy call to Guyana, and one of its helicopters (Sea Lynx I think) flew up our river helping the Guyana Security forces find the Bandar camp.

The Guyana Army later swooped in on them and cleaned them right out of existence, and those who escaped left the area for good. So we did not have to kill anyone, justice was served...and we did not have to put any blood on our hands in the end.

CHAPTER 7 - POLICE ABUSES OF NATIVE PEOPLES

These are just some of the cases I know of personally:

One of my wife's cousins came home covered in bruises, and he complained that some non-native policemen from a Police station near the tribal territory had beat him up and were looking to kill him, he disappeared the next day, and a few days after that his body was found, mostly bones by then, he had been executed with a bullet to the back of his head. No investigation was ever launched to solve his murder. That was my friend 'T'.

I have witnessed with my own eyes a non-native Policeman beating a native boy of 16 years old with a wooden truncheon, and he hit the boy on his knee caps repeatedly, that boy cannot walk without pain to this day, the Policeman was never punished for abusing the minor on his own tribal territory. That was my nephew 'J'.

I have witnessed 2 non-native Policeman at a Police outpost in a mining town take a young native man into the station for questioning, a crime of theft had been committed in that mining town the night before, and the native man who was just walking passed the Police outpost was assumed to be the suspect, purely based on the fact that he was new in town, even though the man had just arrived that morning – so, therefore, could NOT have committed the crime the night before.

His proven innocence did not stop the two non-native policemen (who are known to be racists against native people), as they handcuffed the young native man to the bars of a cell, and took turns beating him with a short piece of a rubber garden hose, demanding he say where the stolen items were and who else was involved, the boy cried out in pain and screamed his innocence ALL day long, he was not given any food or water and was not even allowed to lay down to sleep, or to use the toilet, he pissed on himself, remained chained standing like a slave to the cell door all night, then he was freed the next morning without even an apology. That was my friend 'R'.

I have witnessed a non-native Policeman beating up a small and totally peaceful native man (my friend John) in a Disco, because the Policeman wanted to dance with and fondle his young niece, and John just asked him to please leave her alone, then when Johns sister Rox tried to save her brother from the racist non-native Policeman, the Policeman beat her in her face, leaving her eyes black and blue and her lips burst and bleeding, and her face swollen. That Policeman was never punished for his crimes.

We are also aware of Policemen in every country of Amazonia being nothing more than criminals wearing government uniforms, they are taking bribes to protect the OTHER criminals (drug traffickers, human traffickers, etc) or they are committing these crimes themselves.

I remember once a surveillance operation I financed and participated in because tribal hunters were reporting suspicious activity to me near the border.

So using 2 Walkie-Talkies with a 20-mile range that I had purchased for this 'military operation', we put our plan in motion and set up in the spot where what sounded like cocaine drops by air were being conducted.

After waiting a few days in the area, one morning we heard a small single-engine aircraft approaching, it flew low over the trees, crossed the border with the neighboring country where we were in proximity to, then it circled over a patch of Savanna.

The pilot dropped a duffle bag out of the plane and turned to head back over the border, still flying low over the treetops, and thus off of a radar screen as well.

We kept the bag under surveillance with my binoculars, no one made any move towards it.

Within minutes we heard a motorbike engine approaching, on the back of the motorbike were 2 non-native men, they were in civilian clothes, and they rode a civilian motorbike that was red in color.

The man at the back got off as soon as the motorbike reached the duffle bag and he put it on his back, as the bag had 2 shoulder straps, then they turned and drove away in the direction of the nearest town they had just come from.

I checked my watch, from bag drop to bag collection only five minutes had passed.

We had our own motorbike so once the red motorbike was out of hearing range of ours, but still within the visual range of my binoculars, we followed it, pretending to be civilian motorists ourselves.

We followed and saw the motorbike drive straight to the Police Station in that town, the second man went into the station with the duffle bag on his back but came out less than 2 minutes later without the bag.

A little later a small private civilian transport bus came to the station when the sun went down, we were still keeping the Police Station under surveillance, the bus driver came out of the station with the duffle bag and drove away with it.

We followed the bus to a welder, who closed his shop when the bus drove into his garage.

The next day the bus was driven out and went to pick up goods (no passengers) to transport to the capital city far away, a whole days drive away in fact.

So since there was only one driver on the bus and no risk of civilian casualties, we passed the bus on the road on our motorbike and set a trap at a bridge near to a tribal village I use as a base of operations in this area.

We knew the driver would have to slow down at the bridge, and he had only one lane to drive on to cross the bridge, so we sabotaged it so that the bus would fall off the track into the nearby ditch, just about 6 feet below the bridge level.

So said so done, and the bus fell off the bridge and crashed, the driver was unhurt and we saw him get out and try to help his own situation. This location was 3 hours out of the town.

So since we had hidden our motorbike about 1 km further up the road on the other side of the bridge (ahead of the accident scene), we walked for it and then pretended to be now passing back on our way to the town that was the point of origin for the bus.

Naturally, we pretended to be in shock and concern and we began to help him ferry the goods up from the bus to the roadside, the bus driver then got a cell phone call, and he walked up to the road level above to get a better signal.

I could not hear what he was saying but something about "come immediately" he said to whoever he was talking to, so I took the fast opportunity to look at the gas tank under the chassis, luckily it was cracked open by hitting a large stone in the ditch, and I could see packages were inside the gas tank with gasoline.

So even though I did not actually see for a fact that cocaine was inside the sealed packages in the gas tank, this for me virtually confirmed the rumors I was hearing of the Police in that town receiving airdrops of cocaine from over the border, and being involved with the drug trade and transporting it under the noses of everyone from that border town to the capital city.

Despite all of this, and my frequent confrontations with criminal Policemen and Soldiers in multiple countries, I still took the time to write to ALL the newspapers in Guyana, asking the Government to RAISE the salaries of Police and Soldiers, and raise the pensions of the elderly, and most of these newspapers actually published it, you can easily verify this by doing a Google search online of this same article headline on the next page:

INSULTING NON-NATIVE POLICEMAN ON NATIVE LANDS GETS HIS COMEUPPANCE

The FIRST incident I witnessed of a non-native Policeman acting belligerent on native lands – then getting his ass whipped swiftly by the natives, was on my own tribal land of Pakuri in Guyana, over 25 years ago a non-native Policeman had come into OUR territory, on OUR Heritage Day of all days, and the racist fool cop began to curse native peoples and insult us, saying we were stupid and lazy and all kinds of things, and how he could put all of us in 'our place' sing; openhandedly IF he wanted to.

Well, THAT was the last straw, no outsider is going to come onto OUR land and insult us to our faces – and get away with it, and we don't give a damn WHO you are, even the President cannot bring that shit to us and get away with it.

My own brother in law drank the lat fluid in his glass coke bottle, and walked up to the non-native Policeman and smashed the bottle on his forehead, the Policemans forehead began to bleed profusely and he drew his gun to shoot my brother in law – but quick as a flash another warrior kicked the gun out of his hand, the Policeman's eyes opened wide in fear when he realized he was now disarmed and surrounded by pissed-off warriors, so he ran for his life.

Our then Chief had to catch him and throw himself over him to save the policeman, then the policeman tried to stab the Chief instead of thanking him for saving his life, so when we saw that ALL the warriors had moved in with spears, knives, machetes and knives to kill the Policeman.

However the Chief shouted at all of us to 'STEP BACK AND LEAVE THIS MAN ALONE!

So the warriors stood down, and the Chief walked the trembling Policeman to his Police vehicle, and got into it and fled for his life off our territory.

I was there that day, this happened just before sunset, because one of our best trained native warriors, an ex-soldier from the Guyana Army called Telo, a Lokono-Arawak soldier who had been one of the Guyana Army Soldiers who was sent to North Korea for training, almost mistook me for a member of the Guyana security forces, because my hair was short and close-cropped at the time, and I was wearing a military uniform (because on Tribal lands the Police cannot arrest a native person for wearing camouflage in their own community) even if it is illegal on government lands in the rest of the country, we have our legal rights to limited autonomy recognized even in the constitution.

Telo had rushed towards me with his hunting knife, as he only heard the commotion and had rushed from his home on the other side of the village to do battle.

"ITS ME TELO – DAMON" I told him at the last minute before he stabbed me in the fading light, and we laughed and went to see all the other non-natives who had come in that day – jumping into their vehicles and fleeing in terror...they thought the natives were rising up again, as we had done in 1969 in another part of Guyana – against Police abuses on native peoples there (but in that case the Venezuelan military and the expat white ranchers had tried to use our hatred for abusive non-native Police and fuel a war we would fight while they claimed political sovereignty over us after we did all the dirty work, and create new neo-colonial fiefdoms for themselves where THEY would rule over us instead; so that thankfully failed, or we would have had to end up killing the ranchers next and then had to wage a guerrilla war against any foreign occupational troops instead, as we want OUR freedom from ALL non-natives – not just some of them!).

Nonetheless, I was with the older warriors, and we have about 30 ex-Army veteran soldiers (and several hundred fighting age males) in our tribe, including a demolitions expert, as we really considered the possibility that the Policeman we had just beaten and chased out, would have raised some kind of panic alarm, and a nervous government

– ever fearful of a guerrilla war with Guyanas native peoples, might send in Army units from the base near the entrance to our territory, to crush any rebellious mood we were in...but this would have been a fatal mistake, as we were already planning for that scenario to happen, many people on both sides would have died if the Army tried to use force against our tribe. We are not known to be cowards, and we know our 240 square miles of wilderness like the back of our hands, the Army troops do not.

POLICE OUTFOXED BY A NATIVE PRISONER

On another occasion I remember non-native policemen had arrested a native man in another part of the country, and the police vehicle had to cross a river, but as fate would have it, the vehicle got stuck in the middle of the shallow river and none of the Policemen on board knew how to swim, so even though only knee-deep, these cowards were afraid to get into the water.

The river water was a cloudy white in color almost like watery milk, so no one could see what was under the surface, the native man offered to help because he knew how to swim, so the Policemen took off his handcuffs and told him to dive under the vehicle to see what was causing the vehicle to be unable to move.

The native man dived under the vehicle and after about a minute, he surfaced to say that the chassis was stuck on rocks so he would have to manually try to dislodge them, but it would take him some time. So the Police officers shouted at him and told him to hurry up and do it.

The native man took a deep breath and submerged, a few minutes passed and there was no sign of him...he had swam underwater to the other side of the river, climbed out on the other bank, and calmly made his way to the border a few kilometers away, where he crossed over into the safety of his tribe in a neighboring country LOL

POLICE SWAT TEAM DISARMED, BEATEN AND CHASED OUT OF NATIVE VILLAGE

On another great occasion, an entire non-native Police SWAT team entered a native reservation illegally to arrest someone a rancher claimed had killed one of his cows, well the native guy did kill the cow because it kept destroying the native mans crop farm and the rancher refused to keep it fenced in, despite the native man pleading with him to control his destructive animal.

The SWAT officer woke the native man up by putting an assault rifle nozzle on his face, the native man was sleeping peacefully in his hammock in his house at the time.

"" You bitch we got you now!" the Police SWAT officer shouted in glee – with the gun barrel in the native man's face.

But with a sudden and unexpected move the native man – in his laying horizontal on his back position, kicked the rifle up into the air out of the Police SWAT officers hand – and the native man caught the assault rifle in HIS own hand as it fell back down in the air, and he turned it and pointed it in the SWAT Officers now shocked face saying to him:

"You bitch I got YOU now! ", and the native man walked the SWAT Police officer outside at gunpoint, and told him to order the other officers to lay down their guns or he would blow the lead officer (who he had just captured) head off.

The other officers obeyed, and the native man told them all to get back in their vehicle and get out of his village – and if they ever came back, there would be war.

The SWAT team left all their weapons and sped away in haste, what utter defeat and humiliation was on their faces.

The next day all their weapons were delivered to the nearest Police outpost about 25 miles away with a note saying - "DONT COME BACK".

Never had any more non-native Police try to enter that native village ever again to try to arrest anyone.

Salaries and pensions must be raised in Guyana![1]

This was e-mailed separately (in the hopes that at least one would publish it – and they did) to the Guyana Times, Kaieteur News, and Stabroek News in Guyana on 11 September 2011.

Dear Editor,[2]

I recently spent 8 wonderful weeks in Guyana and talked with Policemen, Teachers and Pensioners (among others), and ALL were adamant about the same issue - they are not getting enough money to survive in present day Guyana.

I don't want to waste valuable space in this respected newspaper by way of voluminous writing, but suffice to say that these few points should be given the highest consideration by our current and future leaders and ACTED upon, not merely pondered or vaguely hinted at - with no subsequent follow-through.

I am told that the average Policeman in Guyana makes less than GY$50,000 (US$250) per month, if he has house rent, utility bills, medical bills, food and other day to day necessities to pay (and he most assuredly does!) how can he support himself alone - or a wife and children! It is impossible, and we wonder why so many officers take bribes; could they survive without doing so in these times? Morally bribe taking in wrong, but when one has bills to pay in order to survive - morals often take a back seat.

I am told that the average teacher in Guyana makes less GY$40,000 (US$200) per month, for the same reasons above - how can we expect to attract the best and brightest to this noble profession - whom we rely upon to lay the foundation for the leaders of tomorrow and future generations?

---

1.   https://www.facebook.com/notes/damon-gerard-corrie/
salaries-and-pensions-must-be-raised-in-guyana/10150361772076251/

2.   https://www.facebook.com/notes/damon-gerard-corrie/
salaries-and-pensions-must-be-raised-in-guyana/10150361772076251/

If I could have my wish come true we would see Policemen and Teachers in Guyana earning a take-home pay of at least GY$100,000 (US$500) per month.

I am told that the average pensioner in Guyana receives less than GY$7,500 (US$37.50) per month, how in our right minds can we expect even a single elderly person to survive on GY$250 (US$1.25) per day on average? Anything less than GY$1,000 (US$5) per day for a monthly average of GY$30,000 (US$150) in pension per elderly person is inhumane. Would any Minister in or out of office give his or her old mother or father GY$250 ($1.25) per day and expect them to survive on that? In a country where a loaf of bread costs GY$200.00! (US$1)

I am not blaming any political party as it serves no purpose to do so, each party has done positive and negative, no government on earth has ever been - or will ever be perfect.

However - we can look at the Amerindian government of Bolivia under President Evo Morales whom I have met in person, I have also met with 8 Ministers in his government when I was in Bolivia as the only person from CARICOM invited (as a member of the Indigenous Caucus Working Group of the Organization of American States/OAS) to be present at the Presidential Palace when the Natural Gas Industry was nationalized in April 2007.

Do you know that the FIRST thing President Morales did when he assumed office was to cut his own salary as President and that of every government Minister IN HALF!

As President Morales said - "too much of the taxpayers money was being wasted on huge salaries for Government officials, and this money could be better spent on the poor instead....we cannot live in luxury when so many are in poverty in our country".

Ladies and Gentlemen, this is the FIRST and so far ONLY case of a President anywhere in the world cutting salaries of top officials by 50% - and it was done by the world's ONLY Amerindian President, he set the example - but will any other of our elected leaders follow? Or will most politicians ensure that their own lives are led in comfort on the high horse while so many who voted for them are struggling to make two ends meet far down below?

Let us all re-examine our own lives and cut down the vine of selfishness while we plant the flower of generosity within our own hearts.

Guyana CAN do it, there are many examples of financial wastage that can make these things possible if halted and diverted.

As brother Bob Marley said "where there is a will - there is always a way".

Yours faithfully,
Damon Gerard Corrie

CHAPTER 8 - RANCHERS ABUSES OF NATIVE PEOPLES

I actually prefer to confront private citizen criminals, as opposed to criminals wearing government uniforms like rogue Policemen or Soldiers, because not only are the private criminals less well-armed than the Military and Police in most cases, but it is easier to get away with using drastic measures to defend yourselves against them, sure they may have the local Police on their protection payroll...but exchanging gunfire with a rancher is less dangerous than exchanging gunfire with a Police or Army patrol. Wounding a member of the Governments Security Forces is a lot more problematic than wounding a civilian who is already breaking the law by what he is doing to you in the first place.

In one case a rancher near the border was hiring native girls from the neighboring country (where I was) and sexually abusing them, and he would tell them the Police were on his payroll so if they ever thought about reporting him – he would see that they were the ones to get arrested and thrown in jail instead, as he would claim they stole from him in his house or any other excuse he wanted to invent.

I Only became aware of it because a girl I knew had returned to the village pregnant, and I had not seen her for about 2 years, she and I were close, and in chatting with her – she broke down in tears and confided to me what the rancher had done to her. But now that she was pregnant he did not want her anymore, and now he was raping her little sister whom he enticed to begin working for him when she had visited her sister a few months prior.

The parents again knew, but felt powerless, because it was not anything the police in their country could do anything about even IF they wanted to, and a complaint had already been submitted to the Embassy of that neighboring country in the capital city of the country I was in, by the girls two old and very poor parents.

I told her parents we could rescue their daughter and any other girl there, but I cannot do everything myself, I needed a group of men willing to help me, as I already had a plan in mind, so several of her male relatives joined me and I set my plan of attack into motion.

We had one old shotgun in the native village, and only 8 cartridges of ammunition, some birdshot, and a few slugs. I got 8 men and I made 9, a holy number in my tribe, so I felt confident.

We put on our camouflaged uniforms, and waited until the sunset, because this neighboring country uses drones to patrol the river border by day, so we crossed the river in canoes in the cover of darkness.

We reached the other bank and tied our 3 canoes to trees at the waters edge, and we used the partial moonlight to make our way silently on the few miles of native footpaths that led to this ranch.

I told my guys the plan one last time to make sure everyone knew what to do, we had all been to this ranch before in daylight, because the previous owner used to buy chickens and pigs from the tribe and sell them other goods they needed, but this son of a bitch running the ranch now, was no friend to native peoples, only an exploiter of them – of the worst kind. So he had to be taught a cold hard lesson tonight.

Luckily we saw that he was already drinking cheap rum and he was already somewhat intoxicated, a little bit more and it would soon be the right time to strike, the dogs were barking and looking in our direction but he maybe assumed it was some wild animal near his property and he was unconcerned.

This man was an ex-soldier himself and had a 303 hunting rifle with a telescopic sight, but that would not be as effective in the hands of a drunken fool, as I calculated on this, so when he had emptied the bottle, about an hour later, and got up stumbling to go inside...I took aim at him with the birdshot and fired in his direction. POW! The old shotgun sounded loudly in the dark as he fell forward into the door, but I knew that at 100 feet away there is no way birdshot is going to kill anyone, at best only make small non-life threatening wounds....it was more for the dramatic effect on the men, as in their minds I had just proved I was willing to kill someone...when in reality I am willing to wound any guilty person, but I have no desire to actually kill another human being. Unless it is really and truly absolutely necessary to save innocent lives.

Furthermore, I needed to stop him from reaching his 303 Rifle because I did not want HIM to kill any of my guys, we were here on a rescue mission, not a suicide mission. So knocking him down in his drunken state where he would imagine that he was hurt far worse than he actually was, which would all benefit us and the operational success odds.

So anyway, he gets hit and falls into the door, he hollers out in shock and pain (mostly shock), and I put another cartridge in and fire up in to the sky (just to create another loud frightening report to keep the dramatic effect going), because that was the signal for the others to rush into the house with kerchiefs covering their faces and rescue all the girls they found inside, they only found the one younger sister so they whisked her out to safety.

The guys said the rancher only had six small holes in the back of his shirt that were not bleeding very much, and he was crawling and talking incoherently. It was just him living there, he had no wife or children, only young teen native concubines he forced to be his sex slaves.

Later found out he had only minor wounds, but the incident was enough to make him sell the Ranch and move elsewhere, we have no troubles from the new rancher who took over.

CHAPTER 9 - INVADING SETTLERS STEALING NATIVE LANDS

You may have realized by now that I don't spend much time talking about anything that I either did not see myself or was not part of myself, I want creative fearless problem-solvers with the guts to deliver justice with their own hands, in their own territories, to use my successes as examples, and adapt and improvise them to suit their own situations.

Some people go around the world recruiting others to join their religions or cults, but I go around the world recruiting timid sheep who want to transform themselves into fearless wolves and defend themselves – instead of waiting on some magical shepherd to come down from the sky to save you and your oppressed people instead.

In a country further away, closer to the Andes than the Atlantic, there was an entire tribe that was having its lands stolen from under them, the civilian non-native land grabbers would pay non-native armed thugs to drive up to the homes and villages and open fire on their houses.

They set fire to the native crop farms, and burned down many native houses as well.

Many native men and boys were beaten up, a few murdered, lots of women and girls raped as well.

However, even though I was asked to help by ONE leader who was still a proud traditionalists, the other leaders were fanatical Christians that belonged to one of these stupid little churches that tell native people who always lived with only the most minimal of clothes covering their bodies, that 'nakedness is a sin', and they made these naive trusting fearful natives they brainwashed, wear long-sleeved shirts and ankle-length dresses 24/7 in the blazing hot amazonian Sun.

Even worse than that, they are so brainwashed into thinking that Jesus said "never fight back – instead, pray for God to fight your battles for you", and they love to quote Pauls crap teaching about "slaves be obedient to your slave masters and submit to your suffering – because our Lord suffered for you willingly".... yes folks, this is how deep and far this colonial tool religious bullshit has infected the hearts and minds of native peoples who once lived as innocent as 'Adam and Eve' in our own Amazonian garden of Eden (and I remind you – even in the Bible it says Adam and Eve were NAKED before they were sinners – and only AFTER they sinned did they cover their naked bodies, so I don't know where you get this crap reverse idea that nakedness is evil and being clothed is holy, that's not what your own holy books said).

Also, our warrior ancestors who ALWAYS defended our peoples lives with FORCE – and who we have to be thankful for our still surviving presence here TODAY, did not lay down their lives just so we would become utter WIMPS unwilling to get off of our praying asses and actually DO something to protect ourselves and our women and children!

So this 'magnificently converted and pacified' tribe was unwilling to physically do ANYTHING to defend themselves....and yet, their deep devotion never made any magical protector come down from the sky and do a damned thing to save them...imagine that!

I mean, what are the odds that inaction would actually lead to a negative end result?

Maybe they forgot that part in the Bible where it says "God helps those who help themselves".

I could not help the bulk of this tribe, and 90% of them now live on the streets on non-native cities, begging for change from passers-by, rummaging through garbage dumps looking for food, selling their bodies into prostitution to make ends meet ....and ALL their lands are now in the hands of the racist non-natives who were persecuting them and using violence to take away what they thought they could successfully use peace and love to retain.

Well, not ALL, of them, the ONE Chief who asked me to help, and who WAS wiling to fight

back, still has HIS land and his people still have their village, they chased all the evangelicals and missionaries out, and they have a room full of posters of REAL native heroes and Defenders from this Hemisphere that I gave him, leaders like Sitting Bull, Geronimo, Tecumseh, Pontiac, Hatuey, and a poster I had made of those brave Mohawk women at Oka facing off against the Canadian mechanized infantry in 1990.

Isn't it ironic, that the only ones who emerged victorious in this years long land battle in that country were the natives who stayed loyal to their native spirituality and ways, and the only ones who lost everything – materially, mentally and emotionally, were the ones who abandoned their ancestor's way and allowed themselves to become brainwashed by non-natives peddling a colonial designed man-made religion....that teaches native peoples that if they want to be good little natives and get into heaven – they should never harm these evil non-native people who are persecuting them, just sit back, do nothing, and pray to God to fight your battles for you instead...why? "Because if you hurt these bad people who are hurting you with violence - God will punish YOU for using violence to protect yourself from their attacks – because God loves you and will silently watch you suffer all your life on Earth and die in misery (while your enemies prosper) – so he can reward you GREATLY when you are dead"....oh man, if that is not the greatest con-game ever invented in all of human history – I don't know what is.

Don't get me wrong, I believe in a divine Creator God of pure love and light, and I pray to it myself, and I am able to help myself and many others with prayers. BUT, I realized long ago, that there is NO way anyone alive can prove to us or guarantee to us, that what the European Churches CLAIMED Jesus said or did, is actually 100% unmanipulated truth, we all know these people were liars to us from the first day we met them, why should we suspend our proven experience with them – to suddenly believe everything they tell us ? Who has benefited the most from their 'pacification religion' us or THEM? Open your eyes to obtain the answer bros.

A NOTE ABOUT INCIDENTS OF MEDICAL DISCRIMINATION

My own first daughter died due to the racism of Guyanese society against indigenous peoples, and my wife had taken our baby to the best private hospital alone, they did not even assign an actual trained nurse to deal with our severely jaundiced baby daughter....a trainee nurse took blood from both our babies arms and both her legs, but the trainee nurse could not stop the bleeding as she had punctured main arteries, and our daughter literally bled to death.

I was away during this time thinking I would get back to my wife in time for the baby to be born with me present, even though my wife told me not to go because the baby could come at any time, I went deeper into the interior trying to track down long lost relatives living near where our ancient Chiefdom once stood. I thought I could have success at rediscovering relatives (and I did) and be there to welcome my daughter into the world as well (but I didnt).

It was without a doubt THE worst day of my life so far, imagine yourself being away when your first daughter was born, then on the day of your return 3 days after her birth, you get the triple whammy news 1 - Your wife had a baby girl 3 days ago, 2 - but the baby died today, 3 - and the baby was buried one hour ago.....I was in a state of shock, guilt, and silence, but I could not live never knowing what my daughter looked like or ever holding her body, so I went to her grave-site, and I dug up her little coffin, opened it, and took out my beautiful little girl, she had such a thick head of hair, and rigor mortis had not set in yet, she was soft and I began to fool myself in my despair and desperation that she was 'only sleeping' ...but after holding her for for a while, I eventually accepted the reality that she was gone and I broke down and sobbed for hours with my wife, my older brother in law Rami, who had faithfully sered with me on all my vigilante justice escapades...had to rebury her for me because I had no strength left....then a few years later I helped to literally dig the grave and bury Rami, with his other 4 brothers and my father-in-law.

Since then, I have had to continue without him, he sometimes still comes into my dreams to warn me if a plan is going to face a danger I have not foreseen as being possible, for that matter the spirit of my daughter also comes to me, and her mum, and her 4 remaining siblings – as well.

News articles & other non-violent actions and resistance

CARICOM MEMBER STATES SHOW CONTEMPT FOR INDIGENOUS PEOPLES AGAIN AT OAS HEADQUARTERS IN WASHINGTON D.C., USA, APRIL 24TH 2012

Once AGAIN – *for the 14th consecutive time* – CARICOM member States of the OAS refused to participate in the meeting at OAS headquarters in Washington DC – of negotiations in the points of consensus, on the historic Draft Declaration on the Rights of Indigenous Peoples of the Americas; April 18-20 2012.

This noble effort could become even stronger than the United Nations Declaration on the Rights of Indigenous Peoples, and WOULD be a beacon of hope for the entire world... if only certain OAS member states would stop trying to sabotage it at every opportunity they get.

As a member of the Indigenous Caucus who has been involved in these important negotiations since the year 2000, I cannot fail to highlight and congratulate the delegations of the following OAS member states from Latin America – who were strong supporters of the hopes and aspirations of the Indigenous Peoples of the Americas; namely:

Bolivia, Ecuador, Guatemala, Honduras, Nicaragua, Panama, Paraguay, Peru and Venezuela. These 9 countries represented half (50%) of the Latin American countries in the OAS.

In contrast, of the 14 CARICOM member states (also half/50% of whom have indigenous populations ranging from less than 1% to up to 13% of their National Populations) only the Bahamas and Guyana attended the opening session – and stayed for only 10% of the time (108 minutes) that the 18 Latin American countries' delegations (who stayed for the entire 18 hour duration of negotiations over 3 days) participated. We would have preferred that the CARICOM member states stayed and at-least 'pretended' to be interested like the 50% of Latin American states who sought every excuse to impede progress...rather than their now routine disrespectful apathy and no-show attitude towards the entire process.

I remind CARICOM that their combined Amerindian Indigenous populations exceed 150,000 persons – with 75,000 (50%) of this amount in 9 Tribal Nations residing in Guyana alone!

Belize has the second highest Amerindian population in CARICOM with 45,000 Mayan Amerindians, Suriname is third with 18,000 Amerindians and Dominica with 9,000 Amerindians of the Kalinago-Carib Tribal Nation. Belize celebrates an official 'Garifuna Day' yet the Mayas who are the actual pre-existing Indigenous people of Belize get no such official recognition. Suriname does not even officially recognize the existence of Indigenous Amerindians within it's borders – yet it negotiated autonomy with the Saramakans – who usurped Amerindian territories in order to establish themselves in that country. This is a gross insult and violation of International Human Rights Laws that even the Secretary General of the OAS referred to with embarrassment at the IV Indigenous Leaders Summit of the Americas in Cartagena, Colombia in April 2012 (though without naming the State directly); and Dominica still refuses to grant more land to the woefully small and inadequate Kalinago Territory in that country – or to remove the illegally imposed Dominica Police station from off the Kalinago Autonomous territory....when they could easily move this hated outpost a few hundred meters and site it OFF the officially recognized indigenous lands. Dominica has & CAN do much better than this sad state of affairs for the descendants of this great Tribal Nation who fought European colonialism in the Americas so heroically for so many centuries!

Would the weak CARICOM states prefer powerful and covetous neighbors to show their Amerindian peoples the respect they deserve? Can CARICOM afford such a political gamble in these times that we live in? Would it not be wiser and more prudent for CARICOM to be on the RIGHT side of International Laws and Conventions concerning Indigenous Peoples and be a positive example in the world – rather than being on their current WRONG side as they hide behind outdated condescending 'National Law'? Is CARICOM so bereft of legal intellectuals that they do not understand and accept that INTERNATIONAL Human Rights Law takes precedence over National Law?

I take this opportunity to remind CARICOM that they once had the praiseworthy foresight to create an 'Indigenous People's desk' within the CARICOM Secretariat – though they have never appointed anyone (and hopefully only an INDEPENDENT Indigenous person would ever be selected – we have enough 'mascots' in member states already) only too eager to take up this seat.

Having both Guyanese Lokono-Arawak and Dominica Kalinago-Carib ancestry myself, and a fearless reputation for holding flames to the feet of ALL governments who violate Indigenous Rights – AND no hesitation to offer praise to all governments who do what is equitable and just for Indigenous Peoples, as well as a reputation for championing Indigenous Rights against all odds that precedes me in every CARICOM state that has Indigenous Peoples....as well as personal recognition within the OAS and consultative status within the United Nations Permanent Forum on Indigenous Issues....many have said that I would be a good candidate for such a position within CARICOM....but my dear friends – it is precisely because I cannot be manipulated by the political power elites that one such as myself will NEVER be considered to fill such an important role.

There are far too many 'yes-men' and women out there who 'put their mouth wherever the soup leaks' (to quote a Guyanese expression) that they would prefer to fill this role...the kind of mascots who will sing the praises of the various CARICOM governments at every local, regional and international Forum in the world and read from the political script given to them – whilst conveniently omitting facts that show otherwise.

INDIGENOUS SNATCH VICTORY FROM THE JAWS OF DEFEAT AT THE OAS, APRIL 23rd 2012

At the 14th Session of negotiations in the quest for points of consensus, on the Draft Declaration on the Rights of Indigenous Peoples of the Americas – held at OAS headquarters in Washington DC; USA – April 18-20th 2012...we (in the Indigenous Caucus) felt a tangible and pervasive sense that many OAS member states had <u>NOT</u> come into this meeting with a genuine determination to make progress; instead – from our perspective in the Indigenous Caucus – we got the distinct impression that many states had come mainly to protect their various regressive Colonial-era National legislation's and NOT bring them in line with progressive International legislation – especially as it concerns the Human Rights of Indigenous Peoples.

Here is but one example of the kind of State level intransigence we had to contend with:

Chief Willie Little-Child of the Cree Nation in Canada (among several other seasoned Indigenous veterans of the Human Rights struggle in the UN and OAS) took the podium on more than one occasion to educate the seemingly unaware State delegates of the following FACTS:

"We remind the States that ALL of your governments have ALREADY recognized the UN Declaration on the Rights of Indigenous Peoples – and supported it in the United Nations General Assembly since the 13th of September 2007. So how can you all sit here and oppose – one after another – language quoted verbatim from the UN Declaration and try to insert language designed solely to weaken THIS Draft Declaration on the Rights of Indigenous Peoples of the Americas? This is supposed to use the UN Declaration as a MINIMUM STANDARD. This is a Declaration FOR the Indigenous Peoples of the Americas – NOT a Declaration for the States of the Americas !

One minute after – we witnessed the States representatives one after another take to the floor immediately following and continue to try to insert language geared to weaken the Draft Declaration.

About half of the current OAS State delegates at this Session seemed to know very little about the previous positions taken by their governments in these negotiations with the Indigenous Caucus, nor do they seem very knowledgeable about the various International Human Rights Laws and Conventions concerning Indigenous Peoples that their respective governments have ALREADY ratified – and are therefore morally and legally bound to respect and uphold.

Though in disbelief, we in the Indigenous Caucus remained respectful in the face of the perplexing attitudes of the State delegates – who's flowery words about their 'commitment to the rights of Indigenous Peoples'...stood in stark contrast to their actions that exhibited a complete opposition to the very 'Rights of Indigenous Peoples' as they are enshrined in International Human Rights Laws and Conventions.

As a member of the Indigenous Caucus who has been involved in these important negotiations since the year 2000, I cannot fail to highlight and congratulate the delegations of the following OAS member states from Latin America – who were strong supporters of the hopes and aspirations of the Indigenous Peoples of the Americas at the 14th Session; namely:Bolivia, Ecuador, Guatemala, Honduras, Nicaragua, Panama, Paraguay, Peru and Venezuela. These 9 countries represented half (50%) of the Latin American countries in the OAS.

I take this opportunity to remind the delegations of the OAS member states that Indigenous Peoples are recognized as 'International Actors' under International Human Rights Law, this is because we represent our Tribal Nations; NOT the Nation States – within who's imposed political borders our Tribal Nations reside.

For example, a Navajo member of this (or any other) negotiation represents the Navajo Nation AS a citizen of the Navajo Nation... NOT as a citizen of the United States of America – within whose political boundaries the Navajo Nation is located.

Former U.S. President Richard M. Nixon was the first American President to officially recognize into Law – the de-facto locally autonomous status of Native American Tribal Nations; and mandate that negotiations between the US governments and the Native American Tribal Nations <u>MUST</u> be conducted on a GOVERNMENT TO GOVERNMENT Basis!

Since the Nation States of the Americas use 'National Laws' as their convenient excuse for NOT doing anything of great significance for the advancement of our Indigenous Peoples Rights within their territories....We, as Tribal Nations should in turn use 'International Laws' as OUR convenient excuse FOR doing everything of great significance for the advancement of our Indigenous Peoples Rights within our own locally autonomous territories.

In this year of Prophecy, the time for the condescending political games that many Nation States have been playing with us for the last 519 years – is fast coming to an end.

It is now time for us to begin preparations for the next phase in our struggle to reclaim that which International Human Rights Laws have ALREADY recognized and enshrined....as our 'inherent and undeniable right to self-determination'. I belong to a Tribal <u>Nation</u> – not to a Nation State!

Neo-Colonialism has replaced Colonialism in this Hemisphere....the conquest of the Americas has not yet ended – and neither has our resistance to it !

SOLIDARITY & CONTROVERSY AT THE 6TH SUMMIT OF THE AMERICAS, APRIL 14-15TH 2012

I consider myself privileged to have heard the following speeches with my own ears – and to be reliably informed by certain political allies in the delegations of certain States of some aspects you will not see mentioned in the media – that transpired during the VI Summit of the Americas in Cartagena, Colombia.

What follows is a synopsis of what I heard from the Spanish to English translators in the Official Conference room :

* President Juan Manuel Santos of the Republic of Colombia:

"I am truly ashamed at the inequality in the Americas...in such a rich Hemisphere...it must not be this way, development flows naturally where equity exists.

Before I came to this Summit I went first to the Arhuaco Indigenous People of the Sierra to seek their advice, for they have a unique way of seeing the world.

They told me 'Mother Nature feels that she has been treated unjustly – and Mother Nature will not remain silent, give justice to Mother Nature now – because it will be very bad for humanity if we don't!'

When I won the Presidency of Colombia – I first made my oath of office before the Arhuaco People – then after in the Parliament of Colombia, I was going to have an open air event and they told me not to worry about the weather "because on that day it will not rain", and indeed it did not, but the next day and for days after we had unprecedented rainfall in Colombia and massive flooding the likes of which we have never seen before. Truly, Indigenous peoples have a spiritual connection to the natural world that we will never truly understand."

> "We have a combined population of over 930 million people in the Americas, we have the best water and food security on Earth in South America; I am told that experts predict that in the future wars will be fought over water."

"We must build alternatives to Colonialism and Neo-Colonialism...and create a new social model that is NOT based on Capitalism or Communism – for they have both been found lacking and do nothing to fulfill the dignity of our peoples."

* President Evo Morales Ayma of Bolivia:

"The struggle for freedom started by our Indigenous ancestors over 500 years ago still continues in the Americas, the most discriminated, marginalized and hated sector in each society on Earth is that of the Indigenous Peoples."

"We have 10 million people in Bolivia, in 2005 when I democratically won the Presidency foreign investment was 600 million dollars, in my 7 years we have increased foreign investment to 5 Billion dollars....this is because we nationalized our hydrocarbon industry. We no longer need to go to the IMF or World Bank to be able to fund Education or Social Welfare programs in our country, before this.... 82% of profits from hydrocarbons used to go to multinationals and only 18% to Bolivia; and we have completely reversed this state of affairs under my administration."

"When we assumed office in 2005 Bolivia had foreign reserves of 1.7 Billion dollars, this after centuries of Colonial and Neo-Colonial rule. In just over 6 years of Indigenous government we have now in Bolivia foreign reserves of 14 Billion dollars."

"Capitalism brings food and energy crisis's...the foreign debt of Capitalism and imperialism is unpayable....it only concentrates wealth in the hands of the few while the majority remain poor."

* Fortunato Rafael Roncagliolo de Orbegoso, Foreign Minister of Peru:

"All of the countries of this Hemisphere once were European Colonies – and all of us carry a great debt to our Indigenous Peoples who suffered the most from European Colonialism, and therefore...the first obligation of a true democracy is the restitution of the rights of the Indigenous Nations that still reside within our borders. If not....then we are 'democracies' in name only, but not in reality."

"We must all support Argentina's rightful claims to the Malvinas Islands"

* Héctor Timerman, Foreign Minister of Argentina:

> *"I was at a meeting with the worlds 300 richest men recently, to discuss 'poverty' and 'women'...so I said to them 'If we are talking about the poor and about women – why are there no poor people or women here?"*

"In Argentina we are still dealing with 19th century Colonialism...how can lands in the Americas still be ruled by the United Kingdom?

40 resolutions in the United Nations in Argentina's favor...is the United Nations for all or just for some?

We must make the uncomfortable comfortable – and the comfortable uncomfortable!"

- WHAT FOLLOWS IS A SYNOPSIS OF WHAT I WAS CONFIDENTIALLY TOLD BY POLITICAL ALLIES:

"On the night of Friday 13th April 2012 things became heated in the room with the Foreign Ministers of the OAS member States – to the point where everyone was ordered out of the room and only the Secretary General of the OAS was allowed to remain with the Foreign Ministers.

The main issues that are creating deepening divisions in the OAS today are as follows:

Despite President Obama's promise on his campaign trail prior to becoming the President of the USA to 'end the embargo on Cuba and restore normal friendly relations' he has instead delivered only a promise of 'change which we CANNOT believe in' since assuming office; perhaps his next book should be titled 'The audacity of False Hope'.

*ALL countries want the American embargo on Cuba lifted –
except the USA which vetoed consensus again.*

ALL countries wanted to re-admit Cuba into the OAS – except the
USA which vetoed consensus again.

All Latin American countries support Argentina over the
Malvinas/Falkland Islands territorial dispute, the USA and Canada
vetoed consensus.

The USA said it has a '*special relationship with the UK*' so it could
not support, and Canada said the Queen of England is the head of
State of Canada as a Commonwealth country so it could not support
Argentina. The Caribbean countries remained silent on the issue, it is
not surprising that the former English Colonies and Commonwealth
states did not support Argentina (*and antagonize the UK*) – for they
depend heavily on tourism and monetary aid from the UK, and neither
did they openly oppose Argentina (*and antagonize Latin America*)
– for they know very well that the UK cannot provide cheap oil or
food to the Caribbean which the increasingly powerful Latin American
block can; so they are sitting on the fence to see which way the wind
blows.

Haiti shocked the Latin American block of countries in remaining
silent on the Malvinas issue, for Haiti was never a colony of the UK,
is not a member of the Commonwealth, and is just a member of
CARICOM which can do little to nothing for it in real terms. Also –
Brazil is the most powerful country south of the USA border and is a
key backer of Argentina on this issue, and Brazil has done more to help
Haiti than any other country in the world.

This VI Summit of the Americas has resulted in a Hemisphere
that is more divided than ever before, though the overt stage-show will
portray otherwise for public consumption, it was a failure unlike the
Indigenous Leaders Summit of the Americas which in comparison was
a resounding success.

Latin America will boycott the next Summit of the Americas if Cuba is not re-admitted to the Organization of American States."

As my plane took to the skies and I left Colombia I remembered with sadness in my heart – the disappointment on the face of Dr. Luis Toro on the last occasion that I saw him at the Summit – before my political allies came to my Hotel room with the info above. The Chilean born Dr. Toro is the Head of the Department of International Law at the Organization of American States – and is the hardest working man in the OAS that I have ever had the honor to meet. To think of all the hard won resources and personal time and strenuous effort of so many dedicated OAS staffers like him who were burning the midnight oil to try to make this VI Summit a resounding success...only to see two countries effectively sabotage the possibility of anything new, concrete or historic – being the end result of it all.

Instead, we witnessed a very grand photo opportunity and heard well crafted political oratories by the Heads of State of the Americas.

INSIDERS' REPORT FROM THE 4TH INDIGENOUS LEADERS SUMMIT OF THE AMERICAS, APRIL 11-13TH 2012 CARTAGENA, COLOMBIA

For the first time in History an Indigenous Leaders Summit of the Americas (ILSA) was given a high degree of prominence by the State hosting the immediately following Summit of the Americas, in 2009 the III Indigenous Leaders Summit had to be held in Panama whilst the V Summit of the Americas (*for the OAS heads of State*) was held in Trinidad. As a Caribbean person I felt ashamed and embarrassed by the insulting attitude of the host Government of Trinidad which only allowed for one person (*Chief Ed John of the Assembly of First Nations of Canada/AFN*) from the III ILSA to address the OAS heads of state for a mere 5 minutes, and only one paragraph in the entire post V Summit of the Americas made fleeting mention of Indigenous Peoples. Despite the valiant efforts of the AFN whic did a great job organizing the III ILSA in 2009, the Political Leaders at that time generally treated the Indigenous leaders of this Hemisphere with contempt.

If this is what can be expected from a Caribbean country – then I honestly hope that no future Summit of the Americas is EVER held in a Caribbean State...with the possible exception of Dominica.

Why Dominica you ask? Because it was Dominica's OAS diplomat decades ago that gave up his seat so that Indigenous Peoples could address the UN General Assembly directly, Dominica also granted it's sole Indigenous Chief of the Kalinago (aka 'Carib') Tribal Nation with a Diplomatic Passport!

The only three issues that stain the name of Dominica in the eyes of the Indigenous & Human Rights world are its inhumane refusal to increase the size of the woefully tiny Kalinago Territory – which is incapable of sustaining the present Kalinago population, it's illegal imposition of a Police Station in the Kalinago Territory against the wishes of the Kalinago people – and in violation of International Indigenous Rights Laws and OAS & UN Conventions; and thirdly –

the fact that Dominica never brought the Policeman who murdered a peacefully protesting un-armed Kalinago tribesman to justice – it merely moved this murderer in uniform to another Police Station in Dominica.

In contrast, at the IV Indigenous Leaders Summit of the Americas in Colombia we were shown a level of respect that I honestly did not expect to witness.

The Secretary General of the OAS, the Vice-President of Colombia, and the Minister of the Interior of Colombia were with us from the beginning; and at our closing ceremony no less than the Presidents of Colombia, Bolivia, every foreign Minister of the OAS – and even USA secretary of State Hillary Clinton herself was present and made a well received speech.

Thanks to gracious sponsorship by the Organization of American States (OAS) I was availed the opportunity to attend the IV Indigenous Leaders Summit of the Americas in Cartagena Colombia, from April 11-13th 2012, I was the only representative for the Caribbean on the Planning Committee and the lone representative of the Indigenous Peoples of the Caribbean present at the Summit. Key people in the OAS know that I function as a de-facto in-house indigenous journalist for the Caribbean and I use my exclusive 'eyes & ears' presence to subsequently write news articles for local, regional and International media – which enables thousands of others to be informed about key OAS efforts that concern Indigenous Peoples.

In my humble opinion, it is a far more valuable contribution for me to function in this capacity in the service of my regional brothers and sisters – instead of merely making verbal interventions that few will ever hear...and even fewer will ever re-discover once interventions become archived for posterity. Indeed I will speak myself if I deem it imperative for me to do so, but at this Summit – there was no shortage of eloquent speakers nor lack of subject areas comprehensively covered (with the exception of the status of our Indigenous Taino Peoples of the

Greater Antilles being officially recognised despite the political status of Puerto-Rico for example), so I listened in order to share now what I heard with all of you.

A SYNOPSIS OF STATEMENTS AT THE IV INDIGENOUS LEADERS SUMMIT OF THE AMERICAS AS TRANSCRIBED FROM THE SPANISH/ENGLISH TRANSLATOR

* Jose Miguel Insulza, Secretary General of the Organization of American States:

> *"I am sad to say that there are still countries in the Americas that do not yet even recognize the de-facto existence of indigenous peoples in their own States – and these countries should do so immediately." (NB – Suriname was not named by the Secretary General, but is one such country within CARICOM that is guilty of this disgrace – a fact that I have been highlighting in my articles for several years – Damon Corrie).*

"In the year 2000 44% of this Hemisphere's Indigenous Peoples and Afro Descendants were listed as 'living in poverty', in the year 2011 – only 30%, so we can see that some progress is being made."

* Ismael Paredes, High Councilor of the National Indigenous Organization of Colombia (ONIC):

> *"It is time for the States of the Americas to stop 'talking' and start 'doing'."*

" 'Poverty' has an entirely different meaning for Indigenous Peoples than it does for non-Indigenous Peoples. For example, the non-indigenous will look into an indigenous home and say that because they have no concrete or tiled floors they are therefore 'living in poverty', but for us indigenous peoples who practice traditional spirituality – we know that having an earthen floor...allows us to enjoy direct contact with the invisible energies of Mother Earth; and this is one of the greatest sources of our spiritual wealth! Our perspectives and

cosmovision are radically different...and the non-indigenous peoples
still fail to comprehend that."

* Angelino Garcon, Vice-President of the Republic of Colombia:

"ALL governments must strengthen local organizations that
safeguard the autonomy of Indigenous Peoples. Indigenous Peoples are
not merely 'NGO's or 'minority groups', they have their own histories,
cultures, languages, spirituality and territories – and ARE autonomous
with their own forms of government; this is a fact all states must be
cognizant of and respect.

There is great importance in these times for dialogue between
States and Indigenous Peoples, the progressive democracy of the
Republic of Colombia has ratified ILO 169 and supports the UN
Declaration on the Rights of Indigenous Peoples...and all countries of
the Americas should do the same.

States have an ethical and legal imperative to ratify and honor these
International instruments concerning Indigenous Peoples."

"When Indigenous President Evo Morales democratically won the
Presidency of Bolivia it was a fiscal basket-case, but his government has
turned Bolivia's outlook 180 degrees....and now it is well on the road to
success; and Colombia wants to be part of this noble effort in Bolivia."

"I am sad to say that criminal violence has led to the death and
disappearance of thousands of Indigenous leaders throughout the
Americas."

"Indigenous Peoples have the right to criticize the governments of
the States in which they live – and NOT be labelled as 'troublemakers'
or 'subversive elements.'"

* Vargas Lleiras, Minister of the Interior of the Republic of
Colombia:

"A constant and respectful dialogue between States and Indigenous
People, it is the only option we have in this Hemisphere as we go
forward into this 21st century."

"For the first time in Colombia's history the President took his oath of office FIRST before the Indigenous Peoples of Colombia – the landlords of this country, and after this he took the oath in our Parliament; this shows his respect and commitment to Indigenous Peoples."

"Indigenous Peoples have an entirely different view and interpretation of the words 'progress' and 'development', and this is why it is imperative that every government maintains the principle of constant communication with Indigenous Peoples in order to obtain their 'free, prior and informed consent' as stipulated in International Human rights Laws and Conventions... this MUST be done before any project that will or may effect them is ever started."

"In 2011, 168 planned projects were discussed with over 500 Indigenous communities in Colombia before anything was done... Indigenous Peoples in Colombia have never been mobilized to such a great extent for dialogue with the National Government in the entire history of Colombia!"

* Jaime Arias Arias, Deputy High Councilor of the National Organization of Indigenous Peoples of Colombia (ONIC):

"We call upon the States of the OAS to honor their commitments and pay their dues to the OAS, only two countries regularly make payments...the other 32 do so only infrequently or never at all; and this is why the OAS often lacks funds to carry out projects that can benefit Indigenous Peoples.

Since these States all deny us our sub-surface mineral rights – which has consigned us to the poverty that we still endure as a result of this inequity...the very least they can do is pay their dues to the OAS so that a tiny fraction of their indebtedness to our many peoples will be able to reach us – like proverbial crumbs that fall off the Lord's banquet table."

* Feliciano, Chief of 50,000 members (25%) of the Nasa Tribal Nation of Colombia (the largest in that country):

"Government spokesmen come before us and give nice speeches, but only ever cosmetic solutions result....never anything serious or equitable for us Indigenous Peoples.

'Internationalism' and 'Globalization'...these are the two key words being used by the Elites of this world to deceive – and which will ultimately destroy all of us Indigenous Peoples!".

* Alberto Achito, a Chief of the Embera Tribal Nation of Colombia:

"Cuba SHOULD be allowed to participate in the OAS...they should not be denied because as the Americans say 'they do not practice Democracy' – but rather should be allowed back into the OAS because the rest of the member states DO! Everyone knows that every country in the Americas continually votes to let Cuba back into the OAS and to lift the criminal embargo.

TRUE DEMOCRACY is not the ritualistic holding of General Elections every 5 years, it is the pluralism of a society – where ALL views are taken into account....not a diplomatic exercise of mob rule where the majority triumphs.

If we are truly democratic societies in the Americas as we love to boast – and none louder than the USA...how is it possible that one country can veto the decisions of ALL others?

Are we living under the rule of an invisible de-facto American Capitalist Empire – where money is all that really matters?

We Indigenous Peoples have our own territories and autonomous tribal governments, and International Law has recognized this fact...yet the rich elites come here to ink deals purely to satisfy their own insatiable avarice....and they give no thought or concern whatsoever for us Indigenous Peoples who will suffer the most from what they do in their private meetings and negotiations."

INDIGENOUS PEOPLES OF THE CARIBBEAN ARE STILL BEING IGNORED...BUT I WILL MAKE YOU TAKE NOTICE OF US...DECEMBER 7th 2012

Dear Editor,

I was pleased to see a documentary on the Lokono, Taino & Kalinago Amerindian Tribal Nations – the first peoples of the Caribbean on the CBC News in Barbados (23rd December 2012), and note that I deliberately said 'peoples' and not '<u>people</u>', because under International Human Rights Laws each Amerindian tribe is a distinct 'people' in it's own right in the legal sense, and though being of the same race – the race has literally hundreds of distinct Tribal Nations that comprise it... all deserving of recognition the same as every other race on Earth.

I notice that the dominant non-Amerindian ethnic groups in the Caribbean today are fond of highlighting how we Amerindians 'were the first to fight against Colonialism' and refer to some of our famous leaders as the first 'National Heroes' in many countries (most notably Cuba), <u>YET</u>– you non-Amerindians do not see that when European Colonialism ended for both of us (Amerindian & Non-Amerindian) –<u>YOUR</u> Neo-Colonialism began for us Amerindians.

History has shown that your valiant anti-colonialism leaders merely put on the attire of the Europeans and continued to deny us – the true landlords of this Hemisphere, <u>OUR</u> right to ALSO be free of the domination of foreign ethnic groups...including YOU.

You bristle when I say this simple truth, not willing to acknowledge that under International Human Rights Laws WE Amerindians have just as much right to have a seat at the United Nations as the political governments of OUR OWN peoples and states as your governments who inherited the theft of OUR lands currently enjoy.

We wish to govern ourselves and not be governed by other peoples the same as you do, but in our case – we wish to enjoy our freedom in the same places we lived before anyone else – and are STILL existing in today despite over 500 years of living under a de-facto armed occupation – disguised as post-Colonial Independence style democracy.

You do not see it this way, but International Human Rights law does – and we have more faith in that than any of your Colonial or Neo-Colonial 'Law Courts', and do not try to sell us the fictitious liberty of citizenship in a democracy where we the first peoples of this Hemisphere will always be outnumbered and outvoted, and where your policemen and soldiers enforce your political will upon us, we are not asking you to leave...

We are not even desirous of secession – we are only asking that our United Nations Declaration on the Rights of Indigenous Peoples enshrined & recognised equal right to self-determination, to live in a manner of our choosing not your dictates in our own territories, be respected; only then can we live in Equity and peace side by side as brothers and children of the one God, is this too much for you to bear?

Many a Neo-Colonial politician has used the invalid argument that 'If we allow you Amerindians to govern yourselves again it will be like creating a State within a state which we will never allow" (Eugenia Charles of Dominica & Forbes Burnham of Guyana said this crap)...to which I answer – so is not the United States of America the STRONGEST country in the world the very one that was founded and is still entirely comprised of many states within the state?

Instead of the current violation of International Human Rights Laws concerning Indigenous Peoples that the Nation States of the Americas are famous for (by denying us our true freedom) – this Hemisphere could become a role model for the treatment of

Indigenous Tribal Nations who have endured over five centuries of justice denied.

CREATION OF THE CARIBBEAN AMERINDAN DEVELOPMENT ORGANIZATION 10 DECEMBER 2012

6 members of the best known three pre-Colombian native Amerindian Peoples of the Caribbean, the Taino of the North Caribbean, the Kalinago of the Central Caribbean, and the Lokono of the South Caribbean, announced the birth of the (non-profit) Caribbean Amerindian Development Organisation (CADO).

The gender balanced CADO Council founder/life members are:

Damon Corrie & Shirling Simon-Corrie (Lokono)
Irvince Auguiste & Loisette Auguiste (Kalinago)
Roberto Borrero & Migdalia Ma. Pellicier (Taino)

These 6 kindred souls are among the best known representatives of their Tribal Nations in this Hemisphere at the highest International levels of the Organisation of American States (OAS) and the United Nations (UN), few others have earned the well-deserved reputations as being dedicated to their peoples by their ACTIONS – not mere words.

We are coming together to bring benefits to our peoples as best as we can. Being traditionalists as we all are, 'Development' is understood by us to be that which restores as much of our tangible and intangible heritage as has been lost and ensuring that as much as possible of it is taken into the future in the hearts and minds of the generations yet unborn that will follow us down the red road of our ancestors

From their spiritual perspective and in their Caribbean traditionalist Amerindian Cosmovision, the 3 tribes are of the same maternal umbilical cord/tree of life, with a base/roots in the Lokono

South, a middle/ solid trunk in the Kalinago center, and top/crown & branches in the Taino North

The CADO motto is: "Dedicated to the Preservation and Promotion of Amerindian Cultural Heritage, and the Implementation of Internationally Recognized Rights of Indigenous Peoples"

These noble-minded 6 have some parting words the world would do well to heed:

"Everyone knows we suffered historical Colonialism's cruel fate first and foremost...

Everyone knows we are the most talked ABOUT but least LISTENED TO of all Amerindian peoples in this Hemisphere....

Everyone knows we are still suffering from present day Neo-Colonialism in our Caribbean that continues to ignore or marginalize our very existence and continued survival...

And everyone __WILL__ know by our historic action on this day that we will __CONTINUE__ to resist our attempted conquest and assimilation – and we shall do so henceforth as one blood, one mind, and one spirit; as our ancestors did before us! For as it was in the beginning...so shall it be in the end.

DAMONS SPEECH TO THE GOVERNMENT OF DOMINICA FOR KALINAGO WEEK 2013

I acknowledge His Excellency the Honorable Acting Prime Minister Mr. Reginald Austrie,

The Honorable Minister of Culture, The Honorable Minister of Education,

The Honorable Minister of Carib Affairs,

His Excellency the Honorable Kalinago Chief Mr. Garnett Joseph and members of the Kalinago Council, and members of the Events Committee for the Kalinago Week 2013 – who sponsored me to be here today;

The Chief Cultural Officer, Professor Lennox Honeychurch, Dr. Alwin Bully, other distinguished guests, ladies and gentlemen of the Kalinago People who have come out in your numbers to show your support here today...

I take this opportunity to raise 4 important points worthy of consideration before I begin...

On the subject of adoptions....

Many Kalinago children are adopted by non-Kalinagos and raised elsewhere, and I think the model of the country of Ethiopia should be adopted here in Dominica, for when a prospective parent adopts an Ethiopian child they must sign a written agreement to raise that child to be aware and proud of its political and tribal nation origins in Ethiopia first and foremost; and this is of vital importance to an indigenous child.

The adopting parents are usually people with only a sense of their political nationality – but not a clue at all about their or their ancestors own tribal nationality of origin, to such people the new political nationality they intend to bestow on their adopted child is all the child needs to know, and all the child needs is for his/her material needs to be provided, enough to eat and drink and wear, toys to play with and a loving home environment....but that is NOT all an indigenous child needs.

And indigenous child MUST be consciously aware of – and PROUD of – his/her tribal TRUE identity! Lets face it, anyone can become a citizen of a political nation....it means very little except on paper, but to belong to a Tribal Nation is something you inherit at birth in your very own DNA, it is in your blood LITERALLY, and it is in your heart and soul...even if you as adoptive parents try to eliminate it from your adopted child's mind. One day he/she will rediscover their spirit...and they may resent you for deliberately raising them to be in a state of ignorance or self-contemptuous of who they truly are.

You who leave your people should also never forget where you have come from, and seek in your adult life to help your people, do not adopt a selfish assimilated mentality – and tell yourself 'my people are the family that adopted and raised me'....for you do NOT know all the facts about the circumstances that caused your biological parents to allow another family to raise their child, so never feel resentment or turn your back on your own people – your tribal nation.

I know also, of several well known adopted Kalinagos who rarely visit the Kalinago Territory, who make comfortable livings abroad and do not send a cent back home to help or support any of their impoverished relatives, and when they do infrequently visit – they never contact the Chief or Council as Tribal Protocol – to inform them that they are visiting the territory, neither do they offer to donate anything or volunteer to do anything that will benefit their people...and usually they only contact their Chief or Council members when they want some favor done to benefit their own selves.....you know who you are....and you need to stop being a 'show Kalinago'...telling everyone abroad that you are 'a proud Kalinago' when your own ACTIONS when you are in your own tribal homeland are no different to that of a self-serving parasite.

You can do better, it is never too late to do the right thing, see yourselves as 'Ambassadors of the great Kalinago Nation' as live as an asset to the collective of your proud and unconquered people!

On the subject of the track record of the Dominica Government in it's treatment of indigenous peoples....

Were it not for Dominica's UN Ambassador giving up his seat – so that indigenous peoples (who were not recognised officially by the UN all those years ago) could address the United Nations General Assembly directly, I daresay that the United Nations Declaration on the Rights of Indigenous Peoples (of the World) might not have been created, or might STILL be a process languishing in the works to this day – not yet achieving the adoption it received in 2007!

Also, as far as I know, Dominica is the ONLY country in the entire world that has granted an official government issued Diplomatic Passport to the elected leader (Chief) of it's indigenous tribal nation....this news has reverberated around the world – and still does to this day!

On the subject of a fair and equitable allocation of Government funds...

It is my suggestion – as I had suggested to the late Guyanese President Cheddi Jagan via a dinner my father had with him on his transit through Barbados en-route to Jamaica for the Ratification of the Law of the Sea; that a percentage of the National Annual Budget equal to the percentage of the National Population that the indigenous peoples represent – in this case 3% of Dominicans are Kalinagos – be allocated to the EXCLUSIVE needs/uses of the Kalinago People, all the current running expenses of the Kalinago Territory including the salary of the Kalinago Chief, the salaries of Kalinago teachers, Kalinago medical staff in the Clinic, Kalinago public works crews, Kalinago Forestry Wardens etc. can be easily covered by such an allocation – and there would STILL be enough funds left for Kalinago entrepreneurs who want to start a new business that would compliment Kalinago Development goals and priorities – to access collateral-free...for this is a problem indigenous peoples from communal cultures who do not hold private land titles – experience all over the world, where they are forced to adapt to the Godless Capitalist so-called 'civilization' imposed around them and ON their backs.

On the subject of a fair and equitable distribution of what everyone knows is Kalinago land – back to the Kalinago people...

I suggest that 3% of Dominica's land area (approximately 9 square miles out of Dominica's 300 square miles) be contained within an expanded Kalinago Territory that has a population that is steadily increasing. The current Kalinago Territory houses about 4,000 Kalinagos on 7 square miles, and with all the miles of uninhabited land on the western border of Kalinago Territory in Dominica's interior (much of which are still de-facto Kalinago hunting territory as it is) this feat can be easily accomplished with the mere stroke of a Prime Ministers Pen with the support of a progressive cabinet. It is not as hard as you may think if you analyse it.

Dominica has done much to right historical wrongs and treat the unconquered Kalinago People with the EQUITY, dignity, respect and appreciation they deserve, but with just a little effort the Government of Dominica can achieve so much more, and these things would secure the government with the vision and foresight to do them – an unassailable place at the apex as the most cited positive example of International 'Best Practices' in the good governance relationship between National Governments and Tribal Governments worldwide.

Now....some people may be wondering about who I am and why I am here, so please bear with me as I attempt to be brief...in laying a foundation in your hearts and minds – as I make my verbal way to the crux of the matter which has led us all to gather here today; with the noblest of intentions to demonstrate initially in word, and subsequently in deed...the fact that THIS government DOES have an equitable vision for the descendants of the first Dominicans.

A proud and free people who's ancestors were the FIRST National Heroes of Dominica – fighting against European Imperialism and Colonialism, by erecting a fitting monument and tribute in their honor – and dedicated to their sacrifices...as many other countries in the Caribbean have already done long ago.

First though, let us examine (albeit briefly) the connections between Dominica and Barbados.

I was born in Barbados but my tribal origins lie elsewhere, just like your most famous historical Kalinago Chief 'Carib' Warner...for he too – just like me – was born of an Amerindian Mother and a white father; on an island separate from where his tribal origins lay.

Like me, he too decided to return to his mother's people and dedicate his life to serving them.

The difference in my case, is the fact that there are both Guyana Lokono-Arawaks and Dominica Kalinagos in my ancestry; so I have dedicated my life to serving both my peoples ...not favoring one over the other...but feeling a genuine and deep love for both.

In 1635 the man who would become famously known as Chief 'Carib' Warner was born in St. Kitts, he was the son of a Kalinago mother from Dominica, and a white father from England – Sir Thomas Warner – who had previously tried and failed to establish an English Colony in Guyana.

The English Governor of Barbados at the time – Lord Willoughby – appointed Chief Warner (who had returned to his mother's people in Dominica and grown into adulthood among the Kalinagos here), as the first British recognised Colonel and Lieutenant Governor of Dominica.

The French captured Chief Warner in 1666, and on 9th December 1667 Governor Willoughby of Barbados negotiated for his release – and re-instated him as Governor of Dominica.

In February 1668 peace was negotiated between the English in the Southern Caribbean and the Kalinago Tribal Nation through the medium of Chief Warner who had the allegiance of all the other Kalinago Chiefs in their Lesser Antilles Territories, but the English colonists in Antigua were exempted – for the Kalinago had NEVER forgotten how they had joined with the French to betray and slaughtered Chief Tegremon and almost all of his Kalinago people there in St. Kitts who had welcomed them to settle to the north and south of his island decades before.

There was no love lost between the Kalinagos and the English settlers of Antigua or St. Kitts – and Chief Warner did not admonish the other Kalinago Chiefs NOT to attack those islands to the north of Dominica, just NOT to attack the other Englishmen in the islands to the south of Dominica.

So Phillip Warner – who was Sir Thomas Warner's second (and pure white) son from his English second wife, sailed to Dominica under the pretext of securing a similar peace 'with his dear Indian half-brother' as the English in Barbados were enjoying, Chief 'Carib' Warner had no reason to suspect his own white half-brother meant him any i'll will, so he welcomed his half-brother Phillip with much fanfare and a grand feast was held in Phillips honor.

Later in the night when Chief Carib Warner and his men were slumbering intoxicated after the party – Phillip and his English cohorts that accompanied him...murdered Chief Carib Warner in his sleep and butchered almost every Kalinago man, woman and child in the Chief's Village that they could lay their savage hands on – with very few escaping alive into the safety of the forests in the middle of the night.

Now here is where MY connection comes in, there has been a persistent rumour for centuries that one of Chief 'Carib' Warner's many sons (from many wives – as was the polygamous Kalinago custom at the time) was later rescued and eventually taken to Barbados....where the ruling class intended to raise him with the intention to restoring him as a grown man in Dominica; to be the Barbados-friendly Governor as his father had been.

However, this plan never materialised and the son of Chief Warner (baptised and registered with the surname 'Warner' in Barbados with no mention of him being an 'Indian' – and giving the appearance on paper – as though he were an English child); remained in Barbados where he grew into manhood and married a local white lady there.

This is how the Warner name survived the centuries in my family until his part Kalinago but white looking descendant Florence Warner (my mother's paternal grandmother) – married Julian Alban Corbin; and the couple had 4 children.

Both Florence and Julian had blond hair and blue eyes – but only one of their children, their sole daughter Pearl (who later married Errie Ward) had the blond hair and blue-eyes of her parents. The three sons (her brothers) had the Kalinago straight black hair and brown complexion that has been a recurring phenomenon in the family ever since the son of Chief Carib Warner became a father in Barbados – over 300 years ago.

My mother's mother was Princess Marian of the Eagle Clan Lokono-Arawaks of Guyana, and the Princess's father was Hereditary Chief 'Amorotahe Haubariria' ('Flying Harpy Eagle') of the Clan, and in the spiritual beliefs of the Lokono-Arawak People, we believe that important things can never remain hidden forever...for the Great Holy Spirit ALWAYS finds a way to bring what was in the dark – into the light one day.

So this recurring evidence of Kalinago features in my mother's paternal ancestry which refused to be obliterated by over 300 years of European genetic infusion and dilution- is to us PROOF that the old rumour is true!

Furthermore, I was never raised to view my Kalinago brothers and sisters as being some 'other' people...NO!

I was always told by my elders that the Kalinago of Dominica are my people just as much as the Eagle Clan Lokono-Arawaks of Guyana are...and I love them both.

In fact, my great uncle David told me to 'go to our people in Dominica' on my first visit here in November 1992 seeking a Kalinago bride, I knew no-one on the Kalinago Territory at that time and I was told that I was the first Arawak person they can recall to have visited them, and they thought that I was very brave to come as a young man among the Kalinago people who were supposed to be my ancient tribal enemies. His Excellency current Chief Garnet Joseph will remember that time as he wanted to interview me, his excellency Chief Irvince Auguiste was ending his second term in office around that time.

I made my first Kalinago friendship with Alvin Thomas (may your soul rest in peace my brother) – who invited me to stay with them, and they offered me every hospitality imaginable.

In late 1992 when people of European descent were for the most part celebrating Columbus...who is a hero to them...but a genocidal villain to us....and marking the 500th anniversary of Columbus's accidental arrival in the Caribbean, and OUR discovery that Europeans existed – and had bigger boats, different diseases and different morals than we did.

So yes, at my then age of 19 I came to Dominica to mark this year of mourning for us by seeking a Kalinago bride to marry – to mark the anniversary with something happy. I stayed for two weeks, unfortunately for me, only on my very last night on the Kalinago Territory – did two beautiful Kalinago girls come to my tent and tell me that they were each willing to marry me....I said to them "But it is too late now – I leave early the next day to return to Barbados"...so I just gave each one a big hug and a kiss on the cheek, and I left Dominica still a single young man.

Because I was unsuccessful my Great Uncle told me to go to our people in Guyana next, and so I did; and during the second week of my two week visit to Pakuri Arawak Territory in Guyana – I met and fell instantly in love with – a beautiful 17 year old Lokono-Arawak girl on 4th December; and on 11th December (just 7 days later) we were married in 1992.

Our 21st anniversary is coming up this year, and we have 4 beautiful children, in fact – I left Barbados on the 20th birthday of our first child yesterday, so that I could prepare and be able to present this speech here today on behalf of the Events Committee of Kalinago Week 2013.

This all takes me back to a fact that I did NOT know about my ancestor Chief 'Carib' Warner, only by reading Professor Lennox Honeychurch's work today I learned about the de-facto Peace Treaty that Chief Warner was able to secure in his time, and I smiled to myself as I remembered the Peace Treaty I created and co-signed with former Kalinago Chief Hillary Frederick in 1999 on the Territory – assisted by fellow Kalinago Jacob Frederick.

For we believe that the driving force in Great men and women that leads them to serve their people..NEVER dies...but lives on in the DNA of their descendants FOREVER.

Of course there was no war between 'Arawaks and Caribs' in 1999, that was NOT the point of it....the reason for my ceremonial and symbolic peace treaty was purely to close and end a sad chapter in the history of our two peoples, and start a NEW and positive chapter in the history of the Caribbean....one where all the old divisions between black, white, brown and yellow – are erased and replaced by a NEW spirit of Solidarity, Loyalty, and Liberty – for AND between ALL of us who share our lands today.

On that note – I return to the main reason we are all gathered here today:

In Arima Trinidad – there is a statue erected by the government to the greatest Nepuyo Chief of Trinidad – Hiyarima.

In Saint Vincent – the government erected a monument to the greatest Garifuna Chief of Saint Vincent – Chatoyer.

In Baracoa Cuba – two statues were erected by the Cuban government to the two greatest Taino Chiefs of Cuba – Guama and Hatuey – with Chief Hatuey (who actually was from the island shared by Haiti & the Dominican Republic today) – with Chief Hatuey being declared Cuba's first National Hero.

In the Dominican Republic – there are 4 statues erected by the government to their greatest Taino Chiefs – including Kaonabo and Anakaona – the first woman Taino Chief in recorded history.

In Puerto Rico – there are multiple statues and monuments erected by the government to their greatest Taino Chiefs – among them Chief Humaco, Chief Hayuya, Chief Agueybana II, and they even carved the face of Chief Mabodomaka into a mountainside AND named a highway after him.

BUT WHERE IS THE STATUE OR MONUMENT TO THE KALINAGO PEOPLE WHO FOUGHT AND DIED IN DOMINICA – TO KEEP IT FREE OF THE EVILS OF EUROPEAN IMPERIALISM AND COLONIALISM FOR THE LONGEST IN THE CARIBBEAN!

The great Kalinago people who fought battles with the Spanish, the French, and the English – but were NEVER conquered or enslaved by ANY of them!

I must admit, I always assumed that there WAS such a fitting and deserved tribute to the first patriots of Dominica somewhere in this country, it was only when the Events Committee informed me that my assumption was incorrect – did I realize that it has been an embarrassing oversight of EVERY government of Dominica until today.

I do not know the Honorable Prime Minister Roosevelt Skerrit of Dominica, nor his predecessor the Honorable Rosie Douglas who had many close friends at University who were Amerindians, but I have only heard positive things about them, and I trust that Prime Minister Skerrit who is about the same age as myself, IS indeed a man of tremendous vision for Dominica and sincere convictions to the Kalinago People.....as we hear evidenced in the words of the honorable members of his government here with us today offering their enthusiastic verbal support for the proposed monument....and I am certain that the Honorable Prime Minister WILL see that this long overdue monument becomes a reality before Kalinago week 2014.

I thank you all for your time.

Written and delivered on 18th September 2013 by Damon Gerard Corrie

THE CREATION OF THE INDIGENOUS DEMOCRACY DEFENCE ORGANIZATION

On 7th February 2015 the Indigenous Democracy Defense Organization (IDDO) was created.

It is the brainchild of Barbados born Damon Gerard Corrie (himself of Indigenous Guyana Lokono-Arawak descent – and well known as the 'radical face' of the Indigenous Rights struggles in the Caribbean region), and it is a Pan-Tribal global entity established to respond to security threats to the Indigenous Tribal Nations around the world; caused by non-democratic occupational Colonial and Neo-Colonial Political Nation State Governments.

'Respond' covers a wide range of courses of action, and Corrie mentioned that it will include as a first response 'the exposure of the threats to Indigenous Tribal Nations in the International media – as well as the official reporting of cases to the relevant United Nations bodies before any further action is contemplated or undertaken...."Human beings are the product of the times and circumstances in which they live, and the appropriate responses in the best interest of the security of the people will be taken at all times by the IDDO"...Corrie said.

Part of what is also being called the 'Corrie Doctrine of vigilante action' that is the foundation of the IDDO, includes the Internationally recognized legal fact that Indigenous Tribal Nations – just like Political Nation-States constructed on and around them without their consent in historical times – have not only a RIGHT – but a moral RESPONSIBILITY to protect all of their tribal citizens from undemocratic or tyrannical occupational regimes that rule over them by force of arms.

If (for example) a military junta overthrows an internationally recognized democratic government in which Indigenous Tribal Nations exist, Article 1 of the IDDO requires the Tribal Governments of any member indigenous Tribal Nations resident in that country – to issue an emergency declaration of 'Territorial Independence' from the government of the Political Nation State in such a scenario (provision is actually made for 'enemies foreign and domestic') if the Internationally recognized democratically elected government of that Political Nation State has been illegally removed from power (and by 'illegally' the text refers to 'any undemocratic means that causes regime change').

However, IF and WHEN an Internationally recognized legitimate democratically elected government is restored in the Political Nation State, the doctrine calls for the Tribal Government/s to immediately suspend the Emergency Decree of Territorial Independence – and resume a harmonious and equitable relationship with the legitimate government of the Political Nation State in which the Indigenous Tribal Nation/s in question resides.

The first and current Chairman of the Defense Commission (CDC) is Damon Gerard Corrie – who is also the CARICOM Commissioner for the Indigenous Democracy Defense Organization (IDDO).

In the IDDO there are also Commissioners for every other region of the world where Indigenous Tribal Nations still survive.

NB – The Indigenous Democracy Defense Organization (IDDO) is entirely funded by private donations and refuses any funds from Political Nation States that may cause a conflict of interest with the important and serious nature of their work to render assistance to the most at-risk and vulnerable Indigenous Tribal Nations worldwide. Membership is free, and the Tribal Governments of all Indigenous Tribal Nations who's existence is threatened by undemocratic regimes – are encouraged to join

INDIGENOUS DEMOCRACY DEFENCE ORGANIZATION BEGINS SELF-DEFENCE TRAINING FOR INDIGENOUS TRIBE IN CENTRAL AMERICA

SEPTEMBER 14-20 2017 – CENTRAL AMERICA

INDIGENOUS DEMOCRACY DEFENSE ORGANIZATION (IDDO) FOREIGN LEGION – CONTINUING ITS LONG TERM COMMITMENT TO TRAINING ITS LOYAL ALLIES IN THE EMBERA TRIBAL NATION HOW TO DEFEND THEMSELVES IN THE PRESENT ERA

Embera children were given a scenario whereby they had only themselves to depend on to protect their tribe (as if the adults were all dead or had fled and abandoned them in a war..what are you going to do – you must learn to defend yourselves and survive, or you must expect to be attacked and die – I told them), they had to learn to work together as a unified mixed gender age varied 'child platoon', to fight barefooted in their normal clothes with handguns & rifles, close range, and long range, in the mud shooting upwards, on rocky hilltops shooting downwards, soaking wet in the rain, or hot and dry in the merciless sunshine, etc, some of these kids have become deadly accurate snipers, the future of the tribe's ability to defend itself will no longer be in doubt when IDDO is finished training them.

Training & weapons costs are being funded personally by IDDO Chairman Damon Gerard Corrie, who was assisted by his second son Tecumseh Corrie (A Pakuri Territory in Guyana born Lokono-Arawak).

Now ask yourself...what is YOUR 'Indigenous Rights' NGO doing to prepare YOU for a worst case scenario in an increasingly militarized and dangerous world..still writing protest letters (and other trivial pursuits) to politicians and organizing street marches and prayerful sit-ins ? Yeah – because that sort of training will REALLY help you in a worst case scenario to save your life...(deep sarcasm).

We are UNIQUE in the Global Indigenous Rights Arena in the IDDO. We train native peoples to be prepared to face ANYTHING and EVERYTHING.

USEFUL LINKS AND RESOURCES TO FOLLOW
DAMONS ACTIVITIES OR CONTACT HIM PERSONALLY

CARIBBEAN AMERINDIAN DEVELOPMENT
ORGANIZATION ON FACEBOOK

https://www.facebook.com/
caribbeanamerindiandevelopmentorganisatioı

INDIGENOUS DEMOCRACY DEFENCE ORGANIZATION
ON FACEBOOK
https://www.facebook.com/
IndigenousDemocracyDefenseOrganization/

https://www.facebook.com/
shamanchief/

Here Damon mentions all the services and tribal products he offers to raise funds to finance all his indigenous rights activities.

https://www.patreon.com/understandingspirituality[1]
    Here is the webpage that handles payments for all the services and products that the FB page lists

Here are the long stay cultural immersion tours in Guyana Damons Clan offers on AirBnB
    https://www.airbnb.com/rooms/
16619252?preview_for_ml=true&source_impression_id=p3_156936756

And here is the day tour combined Adventure, Culture and Nature Eco-Tours on AirBnB
    https://www.airbnb.com/rooms/
25871723?preview_for_ml=true&source_impression_id=p3_156936769

Here is the Instagram account that supports most of these efforts so if you support the author, you can promote this far and wide as a big help as well https://www.instagram.com/eagleclanarawaks/

Or simply look for him on Instagram @eagleclanarawaks

---

1. https://www.patreon.com/understandingspirituality

Don't miss out!

Visit the website below and you can sign up to receive emails whenever Damon Corrie publishes a new book. There's no charge and no obligation.

https://books2read.com/r/B-A-ADZI-NTVBB

BOOKS 2 READ

Connecting independent readers to independent writers.

Also by Damon Corrie

Life Lessons Series
Understanding Spirituality, Anomalous Phenomena as life lessons
Understanding Spirituality, Dreams, Insights, Exorcisms, Visitations
and Shamanic Healing
Dream State Experiences

Standalone
The Amazon is Burning - The Flames of 21st Century Resistance
Inspired by Indigenous Women
Amazonia's Mythical and Legendary Creatures in the Eagle Clan
Lokono-Arawak Oral Tradition of Guyana
Lokono-Arawaks

Watch for more at https://www.facebook.com/shamanchief/.

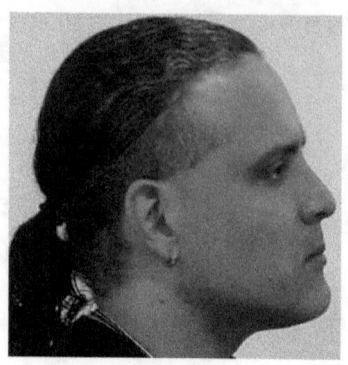

About the Author

Damon, like his 3 older siblings, was born on the Caribbean island of Barbados. His mother Audrey named Damon after the American author Damon Runyon, and from a very young age Damon exhibited a passion and love for writing; however, like most aspiring authors Damon found it impossible to share his manuscripts with a broader audience (until he discovered draft2digital), so for over 3 decades his many works in many genres gathered dust on his bookshelf of unfulfilled dreams.

Damon is a 4th generation descendant of the last traditional Hereditary Shaman Chief Amorothe Haubariria (Flying Harpy Eagle) of the Bariria Korobahado Lokono (Eagle Clan Arawaks) of Guyana, South America, Moreover, the grave of Damon's great grandmother is the only known burial site of a member of Lokono-Arawak nobility in the entire Caribbean - and with a tombstone written in both the English and Lokono-Arawak language, it has become a tourist attraction in the Westbury Cemetery in the capital city of Bridgetown Barbados.

Damon has the gift of premonition dreams and being able to see and communicate with deceased loved ones, and since he married back into the tribe at the age of 19 in 1992, Damon has become the most radical indigenous activists the Caribbean has produced in living memory, and his real-life escapades and supernatural experiences feature in his writings.

Damon was a member of the Caribbean Caucus on the Indigenous Peoples working group of the Organization of American States (OAS) from 2000 to 2016, and helped create the Declaration of The Americas on the Rights of Indigenous Peoples, and he has been a registered participant of the United Nations Permanent Forum on Indigenous Issues (UNPFII) since 2007 (where he also co-mentors international students and writes for the Tribal Link Foundation), as well as being an autodidact journalist with news articles published in 4 continents, and a writer for the Last Real Indians indigenous media website.

Damon (46) and his wife Shirling (44) have 4 living children, sons Hatuey Francis (26) and Tecumseh Shawandase (23), and daughters Sabantho Aderi (20) and Laliwa Hadali, and all live in Barbados. Damon can be followed in Instagram @eagleclanarawaks

Read more at https://www.facebook.com/shamanchief/.

About the Publisher

www.ingramcontent.com/pod-product-compliance
Lightning Source LLC
Chambersburg PA
CBHW060418290526
45791CB00002B/803